The ABC of Sales

The ABC of Sales

Lessons From a Superstar

By Daniel Milstein

How a Russian immigrant with 17 cents in his pocket became one of the top mortgage bankers of all time.

THE ABC OF SALES IS PUBLISHED BY GOLD STAR PUBLISHING

Cover art: M. Salahuddin Khan

Published in the United States by
Gold Star Publishing
A Division of
Gold Star Mortgage Financial Group

Library of Congress Control Number: 2011927195
ISBN 978-0-9835527-0-3　(paperback)
ISBN 978-0-9835527-2-7　(hardcover)
Printed in the United States of America
Second American Edition; April 2012
First Printed in 2011

Ann Arbor, Michigan, USA

www.abcofsales.com

Contents

Words of Praise

"This inspiring book not only tells an exciting tale of success and achievement, it also gives you the tools and strategies you need to achieve all your goals."

—Brian Tracy, Author, The Way to Wealth

"Dan Milstein's success story is an amazing one that is a grabber from page one! His ideas and techniques on how to connect with people are great lessons on sales determination and expertise. Read this book and it will be your ticket to the next level in your sales career!"

—Don Hutson, Co-Author of NY Times International Best-Sellers...*The One Minute Entrepreneur* & *The One Minute Negotiator*, CEO of U.S. Learning, Inc.

"With this book, Dan Milstein will join Zig Ziglar, John Maxwell, Og Mandino, and Brian Tracy in the pantheon of salesmen we should all learn from."

—Jess Todtfeld, Former FOX-TV Producer, President, Success In Media, Inc.

"Dan Milstein is a close friend and business advisor. His book is a treasure chest of information and is an inspiration to me and should be to others as well. While he can't skate, he is one tough business man. When he shoots... he scores."

—Pavel Datsyuk, Detroit Red Wings # 13

"Dan Milstein shows that the American Dream is alive and well for everyone, immigrant and natural born citizen alike. The skills he teaches can be used by anyone to develop their own business and sales efforts."

—Ross Rojek, San Francisco/Sacramento Book Review

"The ABC of Sales is a terrific book about what makes America great. Dan Milstein exemplifies how hard work, unyielding persistence, and a passion for continuous improvement drives success. A must read."

—Joseph Campanelli, CEO and Chairman, Flagstar Bank

"This little book glows with wisdom and a deep appreciation of mankind's ability to make the workplace and life happy, making it a volume that does indeed tell a story of how something great can grow from very little beginnings and also how a philosophy of a gentle immigrant lad can help us appreciate the true American Dream."

—Grady Harp, Amazon Top Ten Reviewer

"Dan Milstein's journey from Kiev to where he is today is a remarkable story. In such a short amount of time he's built a great company while maintaining a sterling reputation. The ABC of Sales will be helpful to anyone who reads it."

—John W. Barfield, Founder, Bartech Group

"Dan's book is a must read. His inspirational story is a journey in overcoming obstacles, as well as a lesson in achieving success. Dan's stories will motivate you to overcome adversity."

—Barry Habib, Founder of Mortgage Market Guide,
Top mortgage lending professional,
Sales/motivational speaker and CNBC/Fox
commentator

"Dan hits the nail on the head. His advice for mortgage loan originators and other salespeople is solid and insightful."

—Douglas Smith, Sales & Sales Leadership Coach,
Author of *Climbing the Ladder of Success*

"Dan is a tremendous businessman and a wonderful person. He always has a smile on his face and has worked hard in life to get to where he's at right now. In this book, his work ethic and determination speak loud and clear for what he has been able to accomplish. I feel proud to call him my friend."

—Katrina Hancock, WDIV-TV Sports
Anchor/Reporter, Host of Sports Final Edition

"This is much more than a great rags-to-riches story. It is a blueprint for success that any motivated professional can follow."

—Matthew Roslin, Executive Vice President, Chief
Legal Officer, Flagstar Bank

"As a supplier of fine food for restaurants and grocers I know the main ingredient to success is hard work and the willingness to go above and beyond the customer's expectations to deliver satisfaction. In 'The ABC of Sales' Dan Milstein demonstrates this principal in many ways. As an entrepreneur I can appreciate his struggles, hopes and aspirations. This book is an inspiration as it proves that in America anything is possible."

—Jim Lipari, Lipari Foods

Dedication

This book is for my parents, Peter and Diana, for having the courage to start a new life in America and thus ensure that their sons would have a better chance to achieve success and happiness, and for instilling in us the most important values: hard work, honesty, persistence and integrity.

It is also dedicated to the loving memory of my grandparents.

X

.

Acknowledgements

It would take a chapter or two to list all of the people who have helped me realize my professional and personal goals and contributed to this book in one way or another. Since that is not a viable option, I will instead formally acknowledge those who have had the greatest influence on my success and privately recognize the many other contributors.

A special thanks to **Stephen Wolpert** for donating an apartment as my family's temporary shelter when we first arrived in America in 1991. The **Keselman** and **Galant** families helped us navigate our first steps in a new country. The **McDonald's Corporation** gave me an opportunity to explore the possibilities of a business management career.

Gail and **Joe Owen,** co-founders of Golden Rule Mortgage, played a pivotal role in my development as an industrious and caring salesperson and provided much of the foundation that led me to establish Gold Star.

I was fortunate to have hired **Brink Cawley** and **Elena Vaduva** as my first two employees. Thanks for having the confidence in a young loan originator who was convinced that we could compete with the "big boys."

Thank you **Rick Richter** and the rest of the Gold Star management team for sharing my vision and helping to turn it into reality, as well as for answering my late night phone calls and e-mails. I am indebted to all Gold Star employees whose dedication and hard work have significantly contributed to the company's success.

We have benefitted from the generosity and loyalty of numerous strategic business partners, most notably Flagstar Bank. I especially appreciate the support and friendship of **Rich Hoffmann, Norm Stepno, Greg Lutin** and **Matt Roslin**.

I greatly value the trusting relationship with my **customers**. My banking career and this book would not be possible without them.

Thanks to my daughter, **Julie,** love of my life for being my number one supporter and bringing me back to reality every day.

I am also grateful to my good friend, **Pavel Datsyuk**. Your funny stories always brighten my day.

In addition, I received valuable support in the development of *The ABC of Sales*. **David Robinson** deserves special recognition for his editorial skills and dedication in assisting me with the creation of this book. It has been a rewarding journey for both of us. I would also like to thank **Mike Ball** for his editorial assistance.

I would like to thank all of the people at Gold Star and elsewhere who shared their stories and offered welcome feedback.

Scott Lorenz of Westwind Communications provided invaluable guidance in the publishing and promotion process.

Finally, I would like to acknowledge all of the talented salespeople I have met during my career. I hope this book will provide further motivation in your ongoing quest to become and remain superstars.

Daniel Milstein

To Reach the Author:

Daniel Milstein
Gold Star Mortgage Financial Group
3879 Packard Road
Ann Arbor, Michigan 48108
Tel 734-717-8600
E mail: dmilstein@goldstarfinancial.com

Preface

As we were putting the finishing touches on this book, a friend who knew about the project said to me, "I can see why you would write about your experiences. But why would you want to give the secrets of your success to someone who might use them to compete against you?"

The answer is simple - I'm happy to share my secrets because there really are no secrets. I'm a born salesman, so what I do is sell. I wake up thinking about our clients, I spend my entire day taking care of our clients' needs, and I go to bed thinking about how we can improve on what we did today and what we can do for our clients tomorrow.

So if someone should learn how I do what I do and then finds ways to do it better, fine! Maybe I'll learn a few things from them.

To get to where I am today I have built a sales organization in which I count on every member to have the same kind of customer focus as I do. This is important, because more than 400 employees and 1,500 of their family members count on Gold Star for their financial security.

But I want every member of my team to be far more than just secure. I want them to achieve as much success as they possibly can and to be happy pursuing their own passions. This makes my organization stronger, and it makes me stronger.

In these pages you will find a lot of information about how to sell anything. In many respects it can be used as a textbook on how to approach the sales profession and how to build a professional sales team. I have also shared enough about my personal journey to help you understand where my own drive to succeed comes from.

Enjoy my book. Learn my secrets. Then go and find your own passion. And - Always Be Closing.

Daniel Milstein

PART ONE
THE FOUNDATION

Prologue

As our plane descended into the Detroit, Michigan airport on December 4, 1991, I remember thinking that the scene below didn't look much like Kiev. The lights were brighter, there were more houses and other buildings of various sizes, and the freeways were crowded.

We were nearing the end of a journey from another world, another lifetime. My parents, younger brother, grandmother and I had flown five days and 6,138 miles from Ukraine through Moscow, to Germany, New York, Baltimore and finally to Michigan. We had arrived in America to begin our new life. But on that cold December night, I wasn't dreaming about eventually being a successful U.S. businessman. Instead, my thoughts were focused on just one thing: surviving.

Chapter One

A New Start in a New World

"To think that a once scrawny boy from Austria could grow up to become Governor of California and stand in Madison Square Garden to speak on behalf of the President of the United States that is an immigrant's dream. It is the American dream."

~Arnold Schwarzenegger

I N MANY WAYS, THE OLD USSR was not an especially idyllic place to grow up. Of course, it was the only life we had ever known, and it didn't seem all that bleak at the time. As the capital of Ukraine, Kiev had many imposing and historic buildings, as one would expect in an ancient city. Then the Communist directives created a city of great contrasts.

During the Communist rule, there were no mansions or roomy condos in Kiev. Our family, like the majority of the other citizens, lived in a basic one-bedroom, 335 square foot apartment situated in one of many five-story brick buildings that dotted the landscape. There were beautiful, ornate churches, but no church services or any other religious celebrations were ever allowed. Every neighborhood had its own familiar convenience store, yet store shelves were frequently barren. Every family had a specific allotment of goods, as a central tenet of the Communist doctrine. The government was quite effective at blocking most of the media coverage of "Western living," so we didn't know much about life outside the Iron Curtain.

School was a central part of our lives, as it was and continues to be for most European children. We attended six days a week and always had a great deal of homework. At the end of each year, we were required to take exit exams before being allowed to move to the next grade. School was especially challenging for Jewish children, which was a major reason my parents stressed the importance of academics. In the USSR, Jews were graded on a difficult curve because of the anti-Semitism prevalent throughout the country. This seemed quite odd, considering that the USSR had been one of the allies during World War II and had liberated the Jews held in the concentration camps. However, it was evident nonetheless, and meant that no matter how well Jewish students performed, only a certain number of us could receive the highest grades. When I was in the fifth grade, I had a study session with a tutor to review a test on which I had received a "C." During the session, the tutor could not explain where I made mistakes, because in fact I had made no errors. It turns out that, I got the C because teachers were allotted fewer good grades for Jewish students. I needed to be five times better than my peers to maintain average academic marks, which is what my parents always stressed.

Because of the arduous school schedule, there wasn't a great deal of "free" time. After classes, we would often play soccer during the summer or ice hockey in the winter in front of our apartment buildings. On Sundays we would finish our schoolwork, then visit my grandparents or occasionally go on a family excursion. While I did not have to work, at 13 I did have a job as a summer camp dishwasher, which required long hours and offered short wages. Because I was smaller than most of the other young kitchen crew, I was able to crawl inside the huge cast iron pots to scrape and scrub the leftovers out.

In a few modest ways, we had what we considered a "normal" childhood.

I also had my first real sales experience, albeit a most unusual one. During this time, food, milk, cigarettes and other popular groceries were typically scarce at local stores, which were only allowed to sell a certain number of each item per day. Even having the necessary coupons didn't guarantee you could purchase the desired goods. One summer when I was 14 years old, a group of friends and I decided that we would become teenage entrepreneurs. We would get up as early as 4 a.m. to be the first in line to buy supplies from neighborhood stores and then wait until 8 a.m. to sell them on the "black market." Walking to a nearby open air flea market, we would display sugar, milk, bread and other essentials that everyone coveted, and sell them for a profit. I usually sold more than my friends, perhaps because I was smaller than them and people felt sorry for me. I prefer to think it was because they were persuaded by my budding sales skills.

I doubt my parents knew about this illegal activity or they would have stopped me. But for us young, seemingly fearless teenagers, it was a fun adventure, a partial escape from the mundane Soviet life. In hindsight, it wasn't a particularly smart or safe job; we knew that if caught, we would likely face severe consequences. Although if we were discovered by the authorities, their punishment would have been less dangerous than the alternative - we also had to worry about the Russian, Armenian and Chechnyan mafia, whose members didn't appreciate competition from novice salesmen. We were definitely in "over our heads" with our business venture.

On the other hand, while I certainly didn't consider it at the time, this did give me an early appreciation for sales.

My childhood was a time of great upheaval in our homeland. The Soviet Union was in the midst of dissolving. We had witnessed the dismantling of the Berlin Wall and were acutely aware of the rumors about revolutions planned to remove the Communist regime from power. They were slowly raising the Iron Curtain, but unfortunately this did little to alleviate the problems my family and I experienced. Jews still were limited in what they could achieve in the former Soviet Union. Public demonstrations against Jewish people made it all the more difficult to gain any sort of meaningful place in the workforce. I remember seeing the demonstrators holding hateful signs such as "Jews Not Welcome" and "Go to Israel" in protest of our way of life. I couldn't understand. "Why do they not like us?" I would ask. It was clear that a person's religion had greater impact than their intelligence and abilities. For example, my father, an engineer, and mother, an economist, had been told they would not be able to attend their preferred colleges and would have limited opportunities to advance their careers because they were Jewish. While I had briefly thought about becoming a doctor or dentist as many of my older relatives were, I learned to avoid developing any real aspirations of being a successful professional.

Chernobyl Explodes

Adding to the USSR's generally oppressive society and inevitable threats occurring during civil unrest, we had the compounded danger of living less than an hour away from a previously unknown town that would become infamous: Chernobyl. During a safety experiment early in the morning of April 26, 1986, reactor #4 at the Chernobyl nuclear power plant suffered a critical meltdown. The resulting explosion emitted searing radioactive steam and nuclear fuel into the air. We lived just 70 miles north of the power plant. I was 10 years old at the time.

My grandfather, a dentist, had been one of the first medical personnel sent to the area to treat the victims. Soon after returning, he died from radiation sickness. My father has also suffered from several illnesses that are directly attributable to the radioactive contamination. The Soviet government tried to cover up the potential dangers facing the area's residents and the selfless volunteers who provided disaster relief. In fact, the government didn't officially recognize the catastrophe until two weeks after it happened. By then it was too late. Thousands of people were affected, including many of the workers sent to the site who were exposed to lethal doses of radiation. More than 3.5 million people were affected by the disaster, and some estimates say that at least 100,000 people eventually died from cancer as a result.

Everyone around us was afraid and people were fleeing to escape the horror. Finally, the Soviet Government ordered all children in a 100-mile radius evacuated to camps near the Black Sea, which was about 350 miles away. It would eventually take several weeks to relocate most of the children to the camps, where they would remain for the next four months. My parents were concerned about the care that I and my three-year old brother would receive in one of these overcrowded, understaffed camps and they decided instead to temporarily move us to Moscow. For the next four months, they alternated in taking extended vacations so one of them would always be with us.

Chernobyl changed my life, but it also taught me an important lesson. It made me realize how much my parents had sacrificed so that they could give their children a better life. It's something we'll always remember. Twenty-five years later, I have my own daughter, and I completely understand at last why my parents made their next major decision.

Planning the Move

It was soon after Chernobyl erupted that my parents began planning to leave the USSR, although they had been thinking about it for some time. They painfully concluded that the life they desired for themselves, and more importantly for their sons, was not possible in our native country. They knew that while the political climate was improving slightly, we would never be able to realize our full potential in the Soviet Union and that moving to the United States was our best option. As part of the October, 1986 peace treaty reached between American President Reagan and Soviet leader Gorbachev, political refugees were finally able to leave the country, although it was not an easy process. My parents told me what they were planning, but didn't share specific details because they did not want me to worry. We couldn't discuss this with anyone, fearful that a friend or neighbor might inadvertently mention it to others, possibly leading to an investigation and persecution by the KGB. It was difficult to remain silent about our planned escape from the USSR, but I knew that I couldn't say a word to my friends or else I might jeopardize my family's security.

It took three long years of careful planning, extensive interviews and background checks. We would sit in stuffy interview rooms and be questioned by United States government officials. Waiting was the most dreadful aspect of the entire process, and I definitely had mixed feelings. I knew we would be leaving and likely not returning to the only home I had known. I was a teenager with many friends and popular at my school. I dreaded the day when I would have to hug my relatives and friends goodbye. However, even lacking my parents' experience and perspective, I knew it was time for us to move to the other side of the world.

Journey to the U.S.

After three years of waiting, the day finally arrived. We were leaving for "the land of opportunity," a country where everything was possible. The night before our departure I was too excited to sleep so I decided to wander around to pass the time. The next morning, Ukrainians would be voting for their independence from the USSR and already there were long lines of people waiting to vote on the referendum. To keep morale high, organizers provided food to the waiting voters. I joined a few friends in the food lines—even though I wouldn't be voting—as if it was my own personal snub at the USSR.

We were required to travel light on our long journey to the United States. As émigrés, we were only allowed to take one large suitcase per person. I packed mine so full it would barely close, hoping to retain as many memories as I could from my home country. We left everything else behind—our valuable heirlooms, books, furniture, toys, clothing…and friends. We said our tearful goodbyes and hugged everyone. Then we surrendered our citizenship documents and passports to government officials. By doing so, we had no way to return to the USSR, not even for a visit. I resigned myself to the fact I wouldn't see my friends again. I was already resentful, and we hadn't even boarded the plane.

My parents had a meager $375 to start our new life, which included $75 for each family member. They were not allowed to take the rest of their savings; the only choice was to give it to friends or the government and the latter was an unwelcome option. I also had 17 cents that a friend had given me to pay for postage to mail a letter back. Because of our political refugee status, that "enormous" fortune and our luggage were all the Soviet government allowed us to bring.

We boarded the plane and tried to relax for the long flight to a place that I knew nothing about and where I had no friends. As the plane left the runway, I stared through the narrow window at the lights of Moscow, thinking about how much we were leaving behind. We would later learn that 90 percent of the Ukrainian voters had supported the measure to secure separation from the USSR. We left the Soviet Union on the last day of its formal existence. My life as I had known it, with all of the challenges we endured – along with my home country – had ceased to exist.

Upon landing in Detroit, I realized how different the U.S. was from what I was accustomed to at home. For example, unlike the few airports I had seen before, where you land and take a bus to a terminal, I was startled when I walked from the plane directly into a waiting room full of people. I am sure that most people are able to tune out the background noise, but to me it was deafening. Everybody was talking and laughing, and I couldn't understand a word. We were not able to ask questions or find our way around in the crowded airport. With the exception of a few universal symbols that we could decipher, none of us could understand signs or even read the letters, as it was an entirely different alphabet. The only things that offered comfort were my parents' voices and the feel of the 17 cents in my pocket, reminding me of my friend who was now so far away.

Our relatives finally found us in the airport and we left for Ann Arbor. As we drove the crowded highway on that cold December night, I thought about all we had given up for one thing: hope. The weather seemed about the same as in Kiev, but nothing else was familiar. We had started a new life, but as a 16-year old, I was definitely unsure of the American Dream.

A local resident had donated a one-bedroom apartment that would be home during the next seven months, until we could move to a subsidized housing project on the opposite side of the city. Our refugee status made us eligible for food stamps and financial aid for the first eight months. The apartment was small for a single occupant, and certainly cramped for five people. My brother and I shared a pull-out couch that we folded up when relatives came to visit. I didn't even bother to unpack my suitcase that first night, instead opting for some sleep after our exhausting trip. I recall that my last thoughts before falling asleep were about the challenge I now faced, and I hadn't been in America for a full day.

Early Lessons

Two days after arriving in the United States, I enrolled at a public high school in Ann Arbor and tried to prepare for the challenges I would face. I had to take two buses just to get there, and because I didn't understand a word of English, my relatives helped me write basic signs such as "Where is the #3 bus?" I tried not to be too obvious, as I didn't need to provide another reason to stand out as a foreigner.

I soon received an unpleasant introduction to American schools and students. My parents had always emphasized that I should try to be five times better than everyone else, whether it was in schoolwork, sports or any other task. While it was difficult for Jews to excel in the Soviet Union classroom, life in the American school system was even more challenging. My classes were nearly impossible because I didn't know what the teachers were saying. I could not make friends because I was unable to communicate with my fellow students. So, I certainly didn't feel five times (or even twice) as smart as my classmates. Young people, and even some adults, were not very friendly to kids who did not speak English. To make matters worse, I had just arrived from the USSR, long considered an enemy of the U.S., and I felt like classmates thought of me as the enemy. I got in several fights during high school, usually the result of someone making fun of me or some other slight.

Because I struggled with the English language, I couldn't take the Advanced Placement courses favored by many other students. One of the classes I did enjoy was auto shop, where I learned the basic skills that enabled me to work on cars on the weekends. Somehow, the parents of a few of my fellow students concluded that because of my part-time hobby tinkering with old cars, I was destined to become a garage mechanic. My parents later confided that one of these people told them, "It is fine if he wants to be a mechanic. That's a good profession too." As they said, there is nothing wrong with being a mechanic; it just wasn't my long-term goal. Some of these former classmates and their parents would later come to me for financial advice, which of course, I enjoyed providing.

In the Soviet Union, we were discriminated against because we were Jewish. In the United States, we felt similar discrimination because we were Russian. From this perspective, the "new life" in America seemed much like our "old life." At times, I felt like I was swimming slowly in a shark tank, but I was determined not to be there for long. One of the major steps I took was enrolling in English as a Second Language classes. While it would be a long while before I was completely comfortable with my new language, after a few months my comprehension and speaking began to improve.

Finding McDonald's

During my high school years, I worked at several jobs in order to help make ends meet. My father and I delivered newspapers and did landscaping for area homeowners. The latter employment occasionally provided much needed comic relief. For example, one summer day, a professor at the University of Michigan hired us to fix the landscaping in front of his house. It was a beautiful Victorian home with several nice gardens surrounding the lawn. Every house on the street was big, beautiful and regal looking. It was difficult to tell where the lawn of one stopped and the other began. We spent several hours working in the hot sun and were making great progress when the professor's neighbor came outside. He began talking with the professor and after some discussion, they both walked over to where we were ripping out a dead shrub. They tried to communicate with us and after a few minutes of hand gesturing, they conveyed that we were also in the process of landscaping the neighbor's yard. My father looked at me with an exasperated smile and we both laughed. We had not understood the properties' boundary lines.

My early dream job was to be a bagger at a local grocery store, which I felt would enable me to buy a used red Pontiac Fiero that I had seen in a newspaper advertisement. (Since then I probably have owned 20 cars of varying types, but never did acquire the Fiero.) My first real American job was at a McDonald's in Ann Arbor, which considering my limited English seemed to be my only option. I was assigned to clean the bathrooms, reminiscent of Eddie Murphy in the movie "Coming to America." It was quite difficult at times, but I always thought of the lessons my parents taught me: "Do every job as well as you possibly can," and "Be five times better than everybody else." I took pride in my job and the company I worked for, even though the conditions were less than desirable.

Since I was 16 and in high school, I had to split my shift in half. I would start work at 5:00 a.m. each day, then rush to school, and finally return to work to finish the last five hours of my eight hour shift. I was up every day at 4:00 a.m. so I could get to McDonald's on time, and often not return home until after 9:00 p.m. Adding this schedule to my homework made for an extremely long day, but I was determined to make it work. McDonald's would give me the chance.

The McDonald's All American Competition in 1992 was my first opportunity for advancement in the company (or anywhere else for that matter) and it led me to what I thought might be a future career in management. Everyone was encouraged to enter the contest, where we would compete on our knowledge of the menu, cooking and other aspects of food service. The winner would be able to enter the management training program and have a better career opportunity. I devoted long hours to studying for the tests; my preparation even included having my parents and brother quiz me. After several months preparing and then taking a series of tests, the winner was finally announced—me! I couldn't believe it. *This is a possible career move*, I thought. During my senior year in high school, I entered the training program and at 18 became a shift manager, responsible for overseeing more than 30 other employees. It was the first time I thought I would have a chance to "be somebody." In fact, working at McDonald's made such an impression on me that I actually painted the golden arches on my bedroom wall. It was an impulsive move but my parents didn't mind. I am sure I was the only McDonald's employee to include the Arches as part of his bedroom décor. It was a sign of the pride I felt for the company that had allowed me to work for them.

To most young Americans, this type of job was a part-time interruption in their daily lives. For me, it was a lifeline, an early opportunity to get a fresh start. Almost 20 years later, when I return to that same McDonald's, some of the employees with whom I worked are still there, and probably still complaining about their jobs. Once again, it shows the value of being proud of the work you do, whether it's selling loans or cleaning toilets.

While I eventually moved away from a career at McDonald's, my time there taught me that I could prevail over the seemingly insurmountable communication gap that plagued me throughout my first years in the United States. More importantly, however, I would eventually learn that this language barrier could be used as an advantage, and not simply an obstacle to be overcome.

Obviously, I don't have pleasant memories of my high school years. In retrospect, it is clear that our move to America was the right decision, but it wasn't easy to see that at the time. Although my first few years here were very difficult, the experience made me stronger and determined to succeed at something. I realized that I could not take things for granted and had to work hard for everything, just as my parents had taught me. Of course, this was small consolation as a teenager, but it would eventually prove to be an invaluable lesson.

My Early Motto: "Be Somebody Some Day"

I knew a college education was a necessary component of success in America, but after graduating from high school, I was uncertain how to accomplish that goal. I decided to enroll at Eastern Michigan University, primarily because it was close to home and relatively inexpensive compared to other colleges. I had no idea that college would take so long and require such a circuitous route to graduation.

In order to pay for college, I took several jobs in the area, including a difficult position as assistant manager of a discount tire store. Changing tires in the frigid Michigan winters was no easy task. Like other working students, I did not have the full benefit of college life, such as living in the dorms and attending football games. I thought of quitting several times—the hectic class schedule combined with early mornings and late evenings at the tire store made life extremely strenuous, and sleep a luxury. To keep going, I would remind myself of the value of a college education and what my parents had given up to provide their sons with a better opportunity. They were unable to achieve their goals in Ukraine, so I was determined to succeed, if only to honor their sacrifice for us.

When I was a sophomore at Eastern Michigan University, I moved to part-time student status so I could find a job with a more promising future. I saw an advertisement for a white-collar position at a local TCF Bank and was hired to work in the consumer lending department. I took a pay cut to be there, but I knew it was the right step to "be somebody some day," which had become my personal motivating statement during this time. However, I had no idea what consumer lending would involve. We had a brief orientation, where several men and women lectured about terms and procedures that I had never heard before. I was anxious to learn, so I listened intently, hoping that eventually I would be able to better understand their directions. I was nervous, but also confident. After all, I had excelled over my McDonald's peers to get the management position and was convinced that I could do it again now.

After orientation, the regional manager took me to the branch where I would work, explaining I would be selling home equity loans. I nodded intelligently and suppressed the urge to ask, "What exactly is a home equity loan?" That first day I also received an unusual welcome from my branch colleagues. I was told there was a call for me, from a well-known professional football player who was interested in a loan. Of course, I was excited at the prospect of handling a celebrity loan on my first day. After taking down the necessary information and consulting with my supervisor, I was informed that the call was staged; one of the others had impersonated the football player. I actually appreciated the humor and later participated in several such initiations of newer employees.

Just as I had done with the language issues that plagued me during high school, I learned to overcome a lack of knowledge by refocusing my energy on other areas. That became the impetus for my eventual career: I had a passion for selling. Finally, I had something I truly enjoyed. I asked questions of my coworkers, watched them and their techniques and took copious notes. I seized every opportunity to improve. While others in my family were doctors, dentists, engineers and economists, I seemed to be a "born salesman." My mother dreamed that I would become a dentist like my grandfather, but once I got a taste of sales, my goal was set. Within 90 days of starting at TCF, I was a top producer for the region.

There was absolutely nothing that would stop me from making a sale. I was relentless in my pursuit. One such instance was a refinance transaction for a married couple, occurring during my first days. It seems as though many customers schedule a family vacation or other trip about the time that their loan is about to close, just as this couple did. The problem was that they weren't scheduled to receive the disbursement check until Saturday, but they were leaving on an overseas trip that morning. In order to satisfy them without breaking any Federal laws, I met them at our branch at 12:01 a.m. on Saturday, to give them their check, thus disbursing the funds on the correct day.

Perhaps I got a little overconfident at this point, because I left TCF after 11 months to be a loan officer at a small mortgage firm. I was convinced that I would be a valuable asset, which seemed a perfectly reasonable attitude. After all, they hired me almost immediately after reviewing my TCF production figures. I felt this was my chance to demonstrate even greater salesmanship. I got my business cards, a small desk, and an encouraging pat on the back from the manager. I was on my own again. Unfortunately, this job didn't turn out as I expected; after three months, I hadn't closed a single loan. I was too impatient. After realizing almost immediate success at TCF, I was under the mistaken impression that every sales job I took would lead me to similar good fortune. As is so often the case, the ability to sell is not necessarily universal across products, much like an athlete's ability to perform in one sport doesn't mean that they will be able to perform at such a high level in a different sport. In hindsight, I failed because I had no direction and lacked the most basic understanding of closing a loan. I would cold call prospects and get their initial interest, but then have no clue as to pricing, rate locking and other fundamental essentials of the loan transaction. Rather than seeking assistance from my colleagues, I became bitter that I hadn't achieved the same triumphs as I did at TCF. In reality, I also missed the infrastructure the bank provided to help its sales staff.

I was still a part-time college student and needed to continue making money to pay for tuition and living expenses, so I took a position managing a branch office of Comerica Bank. We were located inside a supermarket within an obscure shopping center. This wasn't the ideal location for sales success; people came to the store to buy milk and bread, not to obtain a home loan. Once again, I used the lessons I had learned through overcoming the language barrier to achieve success. Our target market needed to be persuaded to stop shopping and come to us for their financing needs. Of course, the benefit to our location was that we had a constant flow of potential customers; we just needed to get them into the financing mindset. We had a seemingly simple approach: blackboard advertisements, free gifts for customers and a great deal of persistence. During the year I was there, we exceeded our sales goal by 486 percent. Not bad for a supermarket loan officer. The senior vice president of Key Bank heard the "buzz" about our sales success and came to my office one day with an enticing job offer—managing the flagship branch at his downtown office. That was a definite boost to my confidence, although I didn't take it because I had bigger plans in mind.

Forgetting the lessons I learned at the previous mortgage firm, the Comerica experience inspired me to think I was ready for greater sales success, so I left to become a loan officer at an even larger mortgage broker firm. As if on cue, I failed again—no loans closed. It took me only four months this time to realize I wasn't quite ready. If I had looked closer, I would have realized that the same issues I faced at my first mortgage firm were still present. I had no direction, was too impatient and made the mistake of "chasing after money." I was still young and had the temerity to believe what I accomplished at TCF and Comerica, I could achieve for anybody, even though I lacked the necessary finance background. Obviously, I was wrong.

Chapter Two
A Few Small Steps, Then Giant Strides

"In the middle of difficulty lies opportunity."
~Albert Einstein

D OES FAILURE REALLY MAKE us better people? I had read articles by management gurus and leadership experts who emphasized that failure is an essential part of success. There are many stories of well-known people who have stumbled once or more only to become highly successful later in life. One of the most inspirational stories (that I had actually learned in high school) highlighted Abraham Lincoln's many setbacks on his way to becoming the 16th President of the United States. He had several business failures, lost seven state and U.S. Congressional elections, and barely got 100 votes in his quest for the vice presidential nomination—before finally being elected President. Of course, Henry Ford is remembered for his innovative assembly line and American-made cars; however his early businesses tanked before he launched the iconic Ford Motor Company. More recently, Bill Gates' first venture with Microsoft co-founder Paul Allen was called Traf-O-Data, also not a big success. Michael Jordan was cut from his high school basketball team. There are many other such stories, which gave me some consolation when I faced my own missteps as a loan originator.

My first two mortgage brokerage failures were major setbacks that I took personally. However, I realized those experiences ultimately could help me become a successful business professional and a better person. It is a lesson that impatient loan officers, insurance salesmen, Realtors, and others who seek to be top salespeople should appreciate. I recall writing brief notes about the lessons I learned during this period. These "essential truths" still resonate with me:

- Don't believe your success will be measured by what you have done before. Instead, it will be gauged by what you are able to do in the future.

- Take any slumps in sales volume as a time to learn more about the business, to reinvent the way you sell and to practice your techniques.

- Impatience can temporarily blind you to your goals. Simply because you aren't doing well at the beginning, does not mean you aren't cut out for the job. It just means you need to be patient and take time to improve yourself.

- By focusing too much on the problem, you lose the ability to find your way to a solution.

Becoming a Citizen

For most immigrants who intend to remain in America, citizenship is a core part of the new life. In 1997, my family reached that much anticipated milestone—becoming American citizens after meeting the five-year waiting period. I recall how excited we were when my father announced that we would begin the process, which would require a challenging written test about American history and culture. For several weeks we sat around the kitchen table and quizzed each other: "What is the first amendment?" "Who was the 12th President?" "Name three people who signed the Declaration of Independence." "Where did the pilgrims first land in America?" At the time, these seemed rather difficult questions that many natural born citizens would not be able to answer. But we did not mind the detailed exam because it was a final step to us being recognized as complete citizens. Because of her age, my grandmother didn't have to take the exam, but she was adamant about joining us. Becoming a citizen would be a highlight of her life. Of course, we were all ecstatic to learn we had passed.

On June 5, 1997 we went to the Detroit courthouse to be sworn in as American citizens, joining a large group of other people of all ages and nationalities. The judge asked us to raise our right hands and repeat the Pledge of Allegiance. I looked around the room and saw that many had tears in their eyes. We all stood and said proudly, "I pledge allegiance, to the flag...." and then sang the National Anthem. It was a brief and simple ceremony, yet so meaningful to those who had come to America by choice.

Avoiding More Roadblocks

After leaving my second job as a mortgage broker, I finally understood what I was missing—a more fundamental understanding of the operations side of the banking business. Yet, although I had hit a couple of roadblocks, I was determined to be successful in the financial services area. In late 1997, I found a job as an underwriter with InterFirst/ABN AMRO Bank. I started underwriting files for properties located in 48 states, for a wide variety of banks and lenders. I was signing off on tens of millions of dollars worth of mortgage loans on a daily basis. This allowed me to learn the operational procedures while meeting numerous experienced bankers, brokers and other professionals, even though I had to take a fairly substantial pay cut to do so. It was an ideal opportunity to improve myself by interacting with some of the brightest people in the banking industry. Once again, I was like a sponge, learning everything "on the fly." I was so motivated that I was doing double the production of any other underwriter at the company while still maintaining high credit quality results. If the company asked me to underwrite 15 loans in a day, I would do 30. If they asked me to underwrite 20 loans, I would complete 40 in the same amount of time. The managers could not believe that I was doing such a high volume without letting things slip, so they randomly audited my work. First they checked just a few files, then a majority of the files, then all of the files. Each time they came back with perfect scores. My fellow employees were incredulous; they could not believe that I was underwriting all of these files with such a high rating.

As one of the faster growing "prime" mortgage wholesale companies, InterFirst was a good place to work. They recognized their success in several ways, including lavish parties for employees and clients. Frequently during the summer months, they would serve frozen margaritas for lunch. One month our production exceeded $2 billion for the first time ever. We were all rewarded with gift baskets featuring various prizes and trinkets. (A personal favorite from my basket was a pair of InterFirst boxer shorts.)

While underwriting at InterFirst, I was simultaneously working as a closing agent for First Plus Finance, a California-based company. By working as a closer, I was able to learn the last step in the mortgage banking process. I was assigned to cover the entire state of Michigan, which involved a hectic schedule. When I was off at InterFirst, I was driving hundreds of miles across the state, often in the middle of the night, so I could close loans for First Plus. The company would send closing documents to my house via FedEx, and my job was to call the borrowers and arrange a time to go to their house in order to close the loan. Anyone who has been in Michigan during February knows that distance driving is no simple endeavor. The weather can be pleasant for most of the day and then quickly turn deadly. I encountered black ice, snowstorms, errant semi-trucks and wild animals as I drove through the night on my way to a closing. I hadn't anticipated such hazardous duty, but accepted it as part of the routine of my second job.

Following The Golden Rule

One day I received a "life-changing" phone call from Gail Owen, who with her husband, Joe, owned Golden Rule Mortgage, a Tampa, Florida-based mortgage company. I was underwriting one of Gail's "problem" loans and it prompted her to call me to see if we could clear up the issues on the loan, as the borrower was in a jam and needed to close. I was immediately impressed by her friendly tone and understanding. Most loan officers with whom I had previously dealt were abrupt and often rude, underscoring the perpetual game of one-upmanship occurring between loan officers on the sales side and underwriters on the operations side. However, Gail was personable and gracious.

My relationship with Gail and Joe continued to develop significantly over the next few months, to the point where we were talking on the phone daily. Through our conversations I began to value the Owens not only as business partners, but also as friends. They treated me as if I was one of their children, and I certainly viewed Gail as my second mother.

I had expressed my desire to get back into the origination side of the business, and after a series of discussions, we decided to jointly open a Golden Rule branch office in Ann Arbor. I was excited at the opportunity to restart my origination career.

COMPLETE CONFIDENCE

"I knew that Dan would be a success. When I met him, he was the most energetic, positive and hardest working person I knew. There was no way he wasn't going to make it. When we opened the Golden Rule office in Michigan, we were going into the unknown, but Dan being the way he was, I knew that it would work. The sky was the limit for him. I was not surprised to see what he would eventually do. He is proof that you can make things happen. "

—Gail Owen, co-founder of Golden Rule Mortgage

An inevitable question is what would I do different to ensure my success as a loan officer? Most important, my experience at InterFirst, Comerica, TCF and First Plus had given me the much-needed operational background; I was confident in my knowledge of the loan process. In addition, I had gained a better understanding of the competition, such as how other lenders were dealing with borrowers. From my first day at Golden Rule, I "mystery shopped" the competition. I detailed the types of questions that customers ask and then called other loan officers to get their responses. This valuable information enabled me to develop a polished script that I would use when talking to prospects.

Turning Obstacles into Advantages

Although I was prepared for challenges ahead, I knew that many clients would still resist doing business with a 24-year old, especially one with a Russian accent. One of our early strategies was focusing on the emerging markets, and I determined that potential customers who were foreigners must feel the same about English-speaking salespeople. So, I decided to emphasize our strengths in assisting these under-served borrowers. Our clients would be able to talk with someone with whom they could speak, relate to and trust. Essentially they would be dealing with their own countrymen. At one point we spoke eight different languages in my office, which sounded like the United Nations during the busy afternoon hours.

In addition, I had developed a rapport with the Russian community, volunteering time to help recently arrived immigrants get acclimated to their new Michigan communities. This would involve driving them to the doctor, finding an apartment, buying a car and other support, the kind of assistance others had provided for my family. This further helped me get established with this growing market. Perhaps it was a communication or trust issue that encouraged immigrant clients to prefer our company, but the result was that people began noticing and calling us. The underlying message is you can turn obstacles into advantages simply by changing how you look at them. It is a lesson that I still apply on a daily basis.

The second pillar of my initial business-building strategy was creating an extensive referral network. Since I did not have a clientele base at the time, I needed a way to compete with the price and costs of loans, so our philosophy became "high volume at a discount." I knew that I could not compete with other loan officers who had been in the business for 20 years unless I found a way to overcome their longevity. So I would provide customers with discount prices and rates. Of course, my commissions would be much smaller, but the plus was that I would make that money back through referrals and repeat business. My goal was to make my clients "customers for life."

First Employees

My first full-time employee was Brink Cawley, who is still with the company and has become a close friend as well. Brink was referred to me by a local real estate appraiser, who told him about a young Russian loan originator in Ann Arbor who was closing a lot of loans. Brink had been a loan officer for about six years, but was considering giving up on sales. He decided to interview with me just to see what I was all about.

From the beginning, we had an unorthodox working environment. When Brink interviewed for a loan officer position, my volume was so high that my three phones rang continuously during our short meeting. He was a "traditional" loan officer who believed the best way to conduct business was at the golf course or on his boat, something many loan officers did. I had to persuade him that being in the office was more important than being on the links. He was coming off a bad year where he only made $40,000, a modest salary he was not accustomed to. I made it a personal goal of mine to get him to the point where he was closing a high volume of loans. We certainly were not short of clients at the time, so there would be no excuses there.

There were many nights when we would stay late at the office, arguing about the best way to advertise, fighting over office supplies and discussing how the office should be run. However, one day during the Christmas holidays, Brink walked in my office and gave me a big hug. I was surprised at first, not really sure why he was being so demonstrative. However, I soon realized it was his acknowledgement for helping him achieve his potential. Indeed, I was extremely satisfied knowing he had regained his sales success; Brink's income quickly jumped to more than $100,000 annually. He offered me a bottle of champagne and we toasted the success of the year. It has since become an annual tradition that we have shared for over 10 years: on the last day of business we share a toast in appreciation of the year's achievements.

Brink is a testament to our business model and atmosphere. Generally when people join us, they don't leave, and Brink is an ideal example. In fact, he still drives three hours round trip each day to work here. When offered new positions with other companies, he politely refused, preferring to make the long trek through rush hour traffic from Grosse Pointe to Ann Arbor. Brink has even turned down offers from me to start a Gold Star office closer to home. He refers to me as his good luck charm.

My second employee was Elena Vaduva, a Masters Degree graduate from Eastern Michigan University who had emigrated from Romania and was working 70-80 hours a week as a financial analyst when she interviewed in February 2000. She had scant mortgage experience, but her unlimited potential made up for that. She was driven to succeed, just as I was, and she made a great income in her first year alone.

IMPORTANT LESSONS

Ten years ago, with job offers from several major institutions in hand, I took a risk on a 24 year-old guy sitting behind a desk in a 300 square foot office, because he struck me as a man who could make things happen. And he has. We are in a much larger office now and clients from throughout the country and overseas come to us for help in financing their homes in the United States. A one-man operation became a two-man operation, and with Dan at the helm it has become one of the fastest growing financial services firms and on the Inc. 500 list. Along the way, I've learned a lot, such as:

- *Don't deal with anything but the "bottom line." Find it and work from there. When faced with a new deal, client or institution, Dan slices through the small talk, chatter, and imagined problems or drama. With the precision of a surgeon, he cuts through the layers of any given situation and locates the heart of the matter.*

- *Deal with flames, not smoke. Don't worry about what could happen. Deal only in what's happening. Be concerned for whatever reality is in front of us. If a problem arises, deal with it calmly and directly. This saves hours of time.*

- *Business is done at your desk, not on the golf course. While some salespeople believe that deals are created over handshakes on the 18th hole, Dan has educated those who work with him that there are better ways to make things happen. He doesn't believe in the inefficiency of spending hours on a golf game to seal one deal. Instead of spending four hours putting around with one Realtor, he suggests buying lunch for all the underwriters at a bank. These are the people who are making the deals happen and ultimately, the customers happy. He is always thinking about the big picture, while intuitively keeping track of how little time there really is in a workday. He believes in making the most of every minute.*

- *Being chained to your desk is not a bad thing if that chain's links are pure gold. Dan always tells employees that the reason he has been successful is that he isn't scared to be chained to his desk. He doesn't see this metaphorical shackle as a bad thing if the end result is growth, happy clients and a successful business. If the chain's links are gold (think efficiency and precision), then that chain has a big pay off. He believes in the American Dream, but understands that it can only be achieved by consistent hard work. He is not afraid of failure because he knows that with discipline and a strong work ethic, he cannot fail. He knows this because he has exemplified it. There are no small jobs in Dan's eyes, only possibility in every ounce of hard work.*

—Brink Cawley, Gold Star

I wanted to show Elena the same treatment that the Owens' showed me, as I felt that it was important that I return the favor. Her first transaction was a construction loan for her sister. We talked to the builder who mailed us the plans. Then we arranged them on our lobby floor to review, using Brink's stapler and my soda can as paperweights. Here we were, a group of mortgage bankers kneeling on the floor in our professional attire, trying to make sense of the proposed building plans. Our diligence and attention to detail paid off. We closed the loan in two weeks and the contractor was so impressed that he has since referred three dozen new customers.

We were very much like a family then. Elena frequently served a huge Romanian lunch that she had prepared at home the night before. We often gathered at the end of the workday to talk about our hopes and plans. The family atmosphere has been rewarding for all of us. It is a tradition that I strive to carry on to this day, even though we are 200 times larger now.

Growing Pains

Unfortunately, at the beginning we still needed to build a pipeline, and revenue was not yet sufficient. I actually lent the office $3,500 from my personal money for the initial start-up costs. Our early marketing budget was $800 a month. My mission was simple: never take a paycheck in lieu of generating more business or helping customers. The idea was that eventually others and I would be rewarded.

In a world of lavish spending by mortgage offices, our 300-square foot space—that was previously used as a closet by an insurance company—was austere by comparison. I had visited origination offices that had large mahogany desks, soft lighting, high vaulted ceilings, and even the occasional indoor waterfall. On the other hand, we were housed in a small office building near Michigan Stadium. There was no art on the walls, the windows were small, the heating was erratic and there was minimal landscaping. But my philosophy has always been to invest in people, not buildings. The "extras" that cost money are better used elsewhere. Then, as now, I would rather invest money in my employees and marketing to grow our business. Later, we did expand the office somewhat, by arranging a small build-out in exchange for a loan done for a contractor who was purchasing a home.

We were certainly creative in generating income during this early period. The office was located near the stadium where the University of Michigan Wolverines football team played most fall Saturdays. They attracted over 105,000 spectators for every home game, so in addition to being situated directly across from tens of thousands of future prospective clients, we had an office parking lot to use. Early on game days, I would place "Park Here" signs around the lot and direct cars to the next spot. Those who have been to a Michigan football game know that parking in Ann Arbor on football Saturdays is not cheap. We were able to make extra cash to pay our rent. Always trying to be one of the "firsts," I believe we were the only mortgage company that used such an "alternative revenue stream" to cover some of our overhead.

We continued to receive rave reviews for the high volume at a discount concept. We were known for offering customers the best possible deals, even though we would receive reduced commissions. While other companies were charging 2-3% commissions of the loan amount, we were only charging ¾ to 1%. Some of our competitors called us the "skinny boys," referring to the thin margins on which we operated.

I recall one client who insisted that he needed to close a loan the next day, a feat that his current lender wasn't able to do. The large builder working on the borrower's house had received the occupancy certificate after months of delay, and now they were under pressure to finish the deal. Closing a loan within 24 hours after taking an application is like expecting a pizza to be delivered to your door five minutes after you place the order. But I was unfazed; I used my underwriting background and all of our resources to get the deal done. The builder was so impressed that he asked me to finance all 82 homes from the subdivision.

More Realtors were hearing about us as well. They wanted to establish a relationship with me so they could please their clients, many of whom were already working with other lenders and bankers. The idea was relatively simple: develop relationships with customers of other originators by offering rates and service that were not available elsewhere. This turned into an avalanche of referrals, and our office grew exponentially. In my first year at Golden Rule I closed 449 loans, quite a contrast to my previous mortgage broker experiences. This was when rates were consistently at 7% and often crept as high as 9%, obviously making it a much tougher sale. Thanks to my enhanced operational knowledge, expanded referral network and the company support, I was among the top 30 of all mortgage originators in the United States, and I was #1 in Michigan, according to Mortgage Originator Magazine's annual survey.

By the next year I was generating approximately $2 million in revenue for the company and closing almost 70 percent of the total volume. However, I was so busy that my assistants were becoming frustrated and even leaving. I closed 94 loans in one month and they couldn't maintain the frantic pace. Some would quit, while others would simply call in sick and never return. It got so busy that I had two title companies refuse to do business with me because they were absolutely swamped in dealing with the last minute issues that arose.

Because our volume was so high, all title orders were rushed and things were often overlooked. The title companies decided they didn't want to deal with the minor mistakes of some of our loans so

THE MILLION-DOLLAR DESK

When we opened the Golden Rule office, I couldn't afford to buy expensive furniture, so we purchased various used items, including my own $550 desk and credenza from a classified ad. During my first year using that worn desk, I earned my first million dollars and continued to expand my production. I later purchased a new desk and Rick Richter (now Gold Star's Executive Vice President in charge of sales) requested that I give him the old one as a "good luck" incentive. He then proceeded to earn his first $1 million. Rick eventually took my second used desk as a "good luck charm," donating the previous one to another loan originator, who is currently in the process of establishing his own track record. Seems like a coincidence, but there is something about that desk. We made a substantial return on that $550 investment.

—Dan

they refused to continue working with us. A few years later, those companies wanted to reestablish the working relationship, but I politely declined. If we were not good enough for them when we were smaller, then why are we good enough now?

Eventually we dropped our turn times on loans to 15 days or less, which was generally unheard of. Most lenders were operating at turn times of over a month, sometimes stretching to two or three months. Volume continued to increase, and I thought that it was time we had more space to spread out. By this time, we had already outgrown our second office to accommodate our rapid growth.

As we continued to expand, I knew the importance of converting from a mortgage broker to mortgage lender status, and in 2004 we acquired our first $5 million line of credit that would enable the company to begin this transition. Now we would need an in-house underwriter and I thought of Andy Newton, who was then at InterFirst. We met in early 1998 when I was assigned to train him and offer support as he learned the underwriting portion of the business, and through this relationship we had become good friends. When I left InterFirst, he was the only person that I asked to come with me. Unfortunately, he respectfully declined at the time, stating that he was content and not interested in leaving one of the bigger banks to join a company with $2,000 in start-up capital. Six years later, Andy called me to once again discuss the underwriting position; and he has proved to be an invaluable asset ever since. We were able to reduce our turn times dramatically by bringing credit underwriting in-house.

Throughout the start-up and early growth of Golden Rule, Joe and Gail Owen continued to offer invaluable guidance.

THE SECOND CHANCE

Dan and I met in 1998 while we are both underwriters at InterFirst. While working there I always wondered what he had going on outside of InterFirst because he was always busy. I later found out that he was working on his other business ventures, while putting in his time at InterFirst. In mid-1999, Dan asked me if I was interested in joining him to start a business as a mortgage broker. Being the somewhat conservative person that I am and not knowing all of Dan's background, personally or professionally, I declined...a big mistake. In April of 2005, our paths crossed again through the help of a mutual business associate. I found out that Dan was looking for an underwriter to help advance his business, so I contacted him. Over the next few months we kept in contact and in July 2005, I was hired on to become the Underwriting Manager at Gold Star Mortgage. Since starting at Gold Star, I found that I don't think I could ask for much more from an employer. From the quality of people that Dan has brought on to the quality of business, the standards have not decreased at Gold Star as it has continued to grow. Dan is one of the most intelligent people I have ever met as well as just being a good all-around person. I am thankful every day for having the chance to work at Gold Star; I just wish I started in 1999 when I had my first opportunity."

—Andy Newton, Gold Star

They provided the infrastructure, support, and advice needed to have a breakout performance. I learned much from them, including the importance of balancing the human side of business with the work side, so I wasn't so much of a "sales machine." A crucial lesson was to find a person or groups of people with experience that are willing and able to act as a sounding board. A well-grounded support network will only serve to amplify a salesman's potential earning power. To this day I have an open-door policy at my office.

THE COGNAC STORY

I had just started working for Dan and he had invited my wife Kim and I over for dinner and drinks. Always trying to make a good impression, I brought a 12 pack of beer, which at that point in my life was the status quo when visiting your boss's home. Dan welcomed us and told us to make ourselves at home. We wandered into the kitchen where we all sat around the bar. Gazing over the bar I realized I brought beer to the wrong party; the bar was stocked only with quality spirits. Wanting to seem very relaxed and confident I asked, "Do you mind if I make a drink," and proceeded to grab a pint glass, fill it with ice, pour a tall drink of what appeared to be some type of whiskey, and then added some coke. The entire time Dan had a huge smile on his face, and I wondered what was so humorous. After I took the first sip he asked simply "How was the $2800 cognac (a gift from an appreciative celebrity client) mixed with that 50 cent coke?" I seemed to choke a bit then, and with a raspy voice said "Absolutely delicious." We both laughed hysterically and that was when I knew I had found a great friend as well as a considerate boss. If the same thing happened while I was working at the large corporate bank, I would have heard about it for months in a negative/embarrassing way. I like to tell this story because it sums up Dan. He takes you for who you are, will let you learn from your own experiences, and is always looking for a reason to laugh. These traits have helped make him and the company what they are: welcoming, non-judgmental, and with open arms, providing unlimited support to make you successful.

—Rick Richter, Gold Star Executive Vice President

Any one of our 400 co-workers is free to walk in, call or e-mail me with questions, problems, or concerns. My goal has been to provide them the same level of support that Gail and Joe provided during my early years at Golden Rule.

In addition to setting personal and office production records, I was reaching another milestone in my life as well. With my grandmother's ever-present encouragement, I was actually graduating from college. Sitting at the commencement ceremony at Cleary University (where I had transferred earlier) in December 2001, I knew other students were undoubtedly wondering what their next steps would be. Some would go to graduate school, others would take extended vacations, and many would begin their careers. I was already a successful mortgage banker managing my own division. By 2001, Realtors and clients had learned about our low rate business plan and the floodgates were opening. I almost had more clients than I could handle and was earning close to $1 million. I certainly knew what my "next step" was going to be.

Chapter Three
Earning the Gold Star

"The critical ingredient is getting off your butt and doing something. It's as simple as that. A lot of people have ideas, but there are few who decide to do something about them now. Not tomorrow. Not next week. But today. The true entrepreneur is a doer, not a dreamer."

~Nolan Bushnell

I BARELY HAD TIME TO SAVOR my much-anticipated college graduation. There was no time for an extended vacation or even a long weekend trip. We were just too busy; the Golden Rule office's "volume at a discount" promise was popular with first time borrowers and experienced homeowners alike. We made less on each individual loan, but were receiving more referrals than ever. It was still a small office, but we knew people were noticing our success.

I also was reaching a critical turning point in my career path. For several years I had been planning to open my own company, and in 2002 I was ready to take on the challenge. Of course, I knew this would be my boldest move yet. I was grateful for all the support the Owens had provided and didn't know how they would react to the news that I soon would leave Golden Rule. "As you know, it's been my dream to start my own company," I remember telling them. "It's been a tremendous experience working with you, but I feel the timing is right for this next big step." I guess I shouldn't have been surprised at their gracious response. "We're happy for you," Joe said. "You and your production have enabled us to retire early." He and

Gail were invaluable as I proceeded with my plans. We agreed that I would stay on for 10 months to ensure a smooth transition. They were kind enough to allow me to switch the signs to Gold Star Mortgage and take ownership of the new entity, without any disruption to our operations.

People often ask me how I chose the name "Gold Star." Organizations often employ expensive consultants to help create a new product, division or company name, yet I wondered how complicated this could actually be. I discovered the answer after considering nearly 100 potential names, and learning each one was already associated with a financial services firm. I was determined not to let this cause a delay in announcing what would certainly be a major force in the lending industry. Impatiently watching the news one evening, I was reviewing yet another series of names when I glanced at my TV and noted that it was a Gold Star Television. I thought this was most appropriate—after all, gold star means "excellence." I always had a goal to associate myself with excellence—in technique, in knowledge, in professionalism, in associates and in a company name. I may have had initial reservations about naming the company based on a TV brand, but felt that as long as few people knew about the naming exercise (until now), my reputation as a "creative genius" was secure.

Soon after, we officially opened Gold Star Mortgage, with the 10 people who were with the existing Golden Rule branch. From their standpoint, it was an easy transition that merely involved new ownership and, of course, a lot of work. I didn't make a speech to announce the plans for our new company; the staff already knew of the impending change. We had a congratulatory lunch and then it was business as usual.

I had 10,000 t-shirts printed with my name and phone number and "Gold Star Mortgage, lowest rates…Guaranteed," and mailed them to our customers and Realtors with whom we worked. That was our initial promotion of the new Gold Star; there were no airplane banners, ribbon cutting ceremonies or billboard announcements. I figured that most of my clients weren't overly concerned about company name changes; they were more interested in results.

We would maintain the same focus—volume at a discount, unsurpassed customer service, and an emphasis on honest, ethical business practice. With a proven business model and a hardworking staff, how could we not succeed? Most of the management team was in their late twenties; I think everyone was probably tired of hearing from the "old guard" how the mortgage lending business was supposed to be run and how loan officers should acquire customers. We wanted to do something new, and our early success gave us a level of confidence and swagger that fueled our approach even further.

BUSINESS CARD PROMISE

The reverse side of a Gold Star business card:

"**Mission Statement:** *Gold Star Mortgage Financial Group is committed to providing the highest level of personal financial services in a professional manner. First and foremost, we represent our clients ensuring they have access to the best rates and a variety of mortgage products. Our high standards provide our clients with mortgage-based savings and increased knowledge to properly manage and control their own financial well-being. Internally, Gold Star Mortgage Financial Group upholds sound management to maintain earnings for our continued growth and provide employees with a challenging and rewarding career. With these principles, Gold Star Mortgage Financial is able to provide our clients with the peace of mind they deserve for years to come.*"

Until this point, most mortgage shops seemed to be "every man for himself" and fee-driven; everything was about how much money you made on a transaction. At Gold Star, we were creating an environment that was supportive, conducive to a team atmosphere, family-oriented, required a dedicated work ethic, and focused on generating loan volume. This approach created a strong bond among the employees. They were goal-driven with the company's and our customers' best interests at heart. It is still a defining factor in what makes Gold Star unique.

Creating a Culture

Early on, I knew the importance of creating a meaningful company culture, although I also knew that it would evolve over time. I believe a company's culture is largely created by its employees, rather than being dictated by a CEO or human resources department.

Ours was a combination of my previous background, the Golden Rule experiences, and a variety of other attitudes and beliefs shared by our originators and staff. Initially, the core ingredients of the Gold Star culture included:

- Passion about our work.
- Put the customer first.
- Positive attitude.
- Open door policy.
- An ethical business.
- Invest in our people.
- A family atmosphere.
- Have fun along the way.

On the outside of our office building we have several framed motivational posters that also speak to our culture. They emphasize to arriving customers and other visitors what is most important to the company and its employees.

CULTURE POSTERS

Putting the Customer first every day—and meaning it.
- *Think of yourself as the customer.*
- *Turning a house into your home, quicker.*
- *Providing the customer with the finest products backed by consistently top-quality service.*
- *Without the highest level of service, the lowest rates don't matter.*
- *Every great business is built on friendship.*

I have since read a variety of interesting books and articles about the value of creating an enduring company culture with which employees can identify. Certainly there is no set formula for establishing one. However, among the wisest advice is to hire people who closely fit the culture. Otherwise, you risk having it diluted by employees who have dissimilar objectives, who don't share the same enthusiasm for the company's short- and long-term goals. For example, we had a veteran loan originator who became frustrated and depressed at the challenging market and his attitude began to affect others in the office. He constantly complained and I could see that others were noticing this as well. After discussing our concerns, we finally realized that his negative attitude did not blend with the company culture. We couldn't afford to have him as part of our team and he agreed another company would be a better fit.

CULTURE: HARD WORK

Dan is the hardest working, brightest boss I have ever worked for. When his employees see him working hard, handling stress, keeping calm when there is craziness in this rather stressful business, it makes those around him try to do their best. Dan does everything fast. He thinks fast, talks fast, helps customers fast, and walks fast so he can get three times as much done as everyone else. He always does it with a smile and he always seems to be in a good mood. His good attitude rubs off on those around him. As part of the Gold Star culture, hard work is expected from everyone. Because we all know Dan expects a lot out of himself and us, we all try to do our best to earn his respect. Dan rewards the hard work with picnics, tailgate parties and special incentives. He makes up contests to make it fun to meet goals and do our best. He also lets you know when you do a good job; sending e-mails thanking everyone for their hard work. He makes us feel appreciated.

—Christi Becker, Gold Star Underwriting Manager

During the last several years, we've talked to several top producing loan originators who for one reason or another didn't complement the Gold Star culture. They may have become top producers for us, but we felt they would not be comfortable here.

Day and Night

In the start-up phase of Gold Star, I was constantly reminded of the Owens' previous support, but we could no longer rely on their highly organized backroom operations. In order to accomplish my never-ending "to do" list, I followed a schedule that was quite taxing, even for someone like me who thrives on long hours and extra challenges. I typically worked until about 9:00 p.m. most nights, then went home to visit with my family and sleep (more like a nap) for a couple of hours. Then it was back to the office to work until morning when I would take a quick nap on my office couch. One of Gold Star's early risers, Runu Chakravarty, would quietly enter my office at about 7:00 a.m., turn on the lights and exclaim cheerfully, "Good morning Dan, another new day!"

I was consumed with organizing all phases of our business: creating employee contracts, establishing loan origination systems, negotiating lender arrangements, and, of course, maintaining my own volume and processing some of my loans. Even though I had many managerial responsibilities, sales was still my favorite part of the day. I would always stop whatever else I was doing to take a customer call. It was an exhilarating, challenging and tiring period in my life, one I clearly relished. I was committed to doing everything possible to ensure Gold Star Mortgage would succeed on a grand scale.

Working nights often entailed late night dining excursions. I would join a few other stalwart employees for a visit to the White Castle "restaurant" across the street. It always amused me to watch the puzzled expressions of the bar crowd and other after hours patrons who probably wondered what these "suits" were doing there. Of course, we felt at home, discussing Gold Star business with each other and waiting for our burgers and fries, so we could rush back to the office for a few more hours of work.

Competitive Edge

We also had to pay close attention to the competition; during this time it seemed that mortgage companies were opening on every corner. I knew that Gold Star had to be different than mortgage firms if we wanted to flourish. In addition to Michigan autoworkers, the emerging markets and the diverse customers who favored our discount pricing, I saw an opportunity to establish a professional athlete niche. It began by accident, when a Realtor called me on behalf of a San Jose Sharks hockey player, who subsequently referred me to his teammates. I later purchased a list of top sports agents and sent them a letter outlining my background, including testimonials from other sports professionals. I met my most memorable sports client in 2001, when the Detroit Red Wings invited Russian hockey player Pavel Datsyuk for a tryout. Although most agents and other "experts" initially doubted he had much of a long-term pro future, on the second day of Pavel's tryout, the team concluded he was worth their investment and offered him a three-year contract. When I met Pavel, he didn't speak English, had no American credit and needed a place to live. Based on my lender relationships, I was able to help him get a loan for his first home, for which he was extremely grateful. Pavel has since gained a reputation as one of the NHL's top players, helped his team win two Stanley cups and become one of my good friends as well.

I learned that not all sports figures are wealthy or ideal clients. According to a *Sports Illustrated* article, 80 percent of NFL players file for bankruptcy two years after they retire. About 60 percent of NBA players do the same five years after they stop playing. So I probably shouldn't have been surprised when an agent and financial planner asked me to help their NFL player-client who had a new $30 million contract with a $6 million upfront signing bonus, along with one of the lowest credit scores I had ever seen, resulting from non-payment of judgments and collections. He just didn't believe in paying bills. I explained that helping him obtain a mortgage would be a true test of my expertise. I called several banks to ask if they would do a private loan in exchange for him appearing in commercials to endorse their company. No deal. I wasn't willing to give up and after exhausting several other options, finally found a lender that was willing to make the loan for a grateful, credit-impaired football player.

LEARNING CURVE LESSONS

There were several lessons during the start-up of Gold Star that could be added to a "How-to Manual for Starting a New Company." For example:

1. *Carefully evaluate all options before outsourcing critical operational functions, such as financial management. We initially contracted with a CPA to oversee the company's books. However, we missed having someone dedicated solely to our business and it turned out to be more expensive than an in-house financial officer.*

2. *Constantly adjust your operational plans and maintain the ability to make quick decisions to expedite essential changes.*

3. *Be conservative in hiring. We were extremely busy during those first several months, but hesitated to make additional hires until we were convinced production would remain at sufficient levels to ensure their long-term employment.*

4. *Set money aside for slower periods. While many loan originators couldn't wait to spend their commissions on a new car, expensive vacations and other necessities, I knew I might have to eventually invest my own funds in the company's future.*

5. *Develop business plans for achieving one, three and five-year goals. Modify the plans on a regular basis.*

I also had an experience that reinforced my belief that some older customers aren't overly enthusiastic about working with younger loan officers. I had arranged several loans for a former All Star and Hall of Fame baseball player. We had completed these transactions over the phone and it was three years before we actually met. When I did get together with this well-known sports figure to discuss another loan, he smiled and commented, "I didn't know how young you were. If I had, I probably wouldn't have given you the chance to arrange my home financing." Obviously, my performance made him realize he had made a wise choice.

We later added teachers, policemen, firefighters and military personnel to our growing list of special interest customers. In addition, we developed a reputation for working difficult loans, those that other originators weren't experienced enough to handle. While our preference is to serve the "best of the best" customers, I knew by assisting Realtors with their "turn-down" loans, we would further underscore our reputation as the experts, and referrals would increase exponentially. Many originators get themselves in a bind by offering unrealistic expectations to agents who promise future business. My underwriting background enabled me to quickly assess the feasibility of challenging loans; thus I didn't damage our reputation by missing deadlines for impossible deals.

Brainstorming

Initially, we held most of our employee meetings at a nearby restaurant-pub rather than a formal office conference room. This seemed perfectly natural at the time, offering an ideal opportunity to brainstorm ideas and implement them on the "turn of a dime," while enjoying refreshments and camaraderie in an informal atmosphere. For example, a few of the hot topics considered during these night weekly conferences:

- Hiring practices
- Complex transactions—troubleshooting difficult loans
- New marketing strategies
- The challenges of growing a young business
- The challenges of our major league sports teams

Obviously, some ideas never made it off the drawing board or cocktail napkin; however the open forum enabled all employees to voice their opinions, which we would then consider and make the appropriate management decisions. The value of these brain trust planning sessions is that we got objective viewpoints and occasionally great ideas that we could then run with. In these informal meetings, nothing was out of bounds; they were a safe place for free flowing ideas - and even a few laughs.

Unexpected Growth

After about six months, the Gold Star infrastructure was in place and we were generating a healthy volume. I was content to have the company grow methodically. A key part of our strategic plan was to extend our reach from a local/regional to more national basis, with initial plans for doing business in at least 20 states. Although there was no immediate rush to expand beyond our main office, two significant events occurred to help make Gold Star a multi-office company and prepare us for even more dramatic expansion in the future.

PERSISTENCE

I quickly realized that persistence is both required and respected at Gold Star. As an account executive at JP Morgan Chase, I wanted the opportunity to work with Gold Star and Dan Milstein, who was ranked in the top 30 loan originators in the country. When I first met Dan in his office, he was on the phone, busily talking to a succession of customers, lenders and others. I said that I would be most interested in assisting him and his customers. He was polite, but noncommittal about my getting any Gold Star business. He explained they already had a sufficient number of lenders and weren't ready to add another one. Of course, I wouldn't give up. Once a week, I drove an hour to Gold Star headquarters, usually bringing breakfast or cookies, sometimes seeing Dan and more often not, but always leaving without any indication that I could add Gold Star to my account list. Eventually, my Chase manager strongly suggested that I give up on what seemed to be a lost cause. However, I continued showing up at the Gold Star offices, somehow convinced that I would succeed. About a year (and 50 batches of cookies) after our first meeting, Dan finally agreed to let me work with his customers on a trial basis. Gold Star soon became my biggest and most important account.

—Tina Jablonski, JP Morgan Chase Bank

In 2004, my processor announced she and her husband were moving to Tyler, Texas, but wanted to remain employed with Gold Star. She wondered if we were interested in opening an office there. I was unsure only because it wasn't part of our immediate plans and we had greater priorities. However, I was impressed with her work ethic and desire to stay with Gold Star. So we provided her with a crash course in the sales side, enabling her to open a home office when she arrived in Tyler. After working from her home office for a few months, she eventually developed sufficient business to make it worthwhile for us to open a small Gold Star branch, which helped us develop a model that we would adapt to other areas.

In 2006, we made a major move that helped propel Gold Star into an even more visible position on the mortgage industry map. The manager of the Allied Home Finance office approached me to discuss potential merger plans with the local Chase Bank branch. They had been asking for suggestions regarding high producing mortgage brokers and were encouraged to call me. Their goals were to be able to close loans in multiple states, and to combine a top producing mortgage brokerage with a correspondent operation. I was intrigued, but in no rush to affiliate with other firms unless I could be assured we would avoid the stumbling blocks often associated with such corporate marriages. We began a series of discussions to see if we had similar long-term objectives, whether such a merger made sense to all of us.

Our casual conversations soon evolved into serious planning to achieve the ambitious goal of uniting the three firms into a single entity. I was excited about the prospects of this potential expansion, but our future certainly wasn't dependent on the deal. We had a successful office of 20 talented, loyal people who enjoyed working with each other to ensure Gold Star had a bright future. I reasoned that if this merger didn't work out, there would be other equally promising opportunities.

Our deliberations lasted more than four months, during which we reviewed mutual goals, financial arrangements and various other topics. Chase's experienced loan officers had to be convinced it was to their advantage to join us. In order to get a consensus, so that everyone would be enthusiastic about joining the new group, I had more than 30 group and one-on-one meetings, where I could share the company philosophy and help make the originators comfortable with the proposed alliance. We finally agreed to the creation of a separate division of Gold Star Mortgage— National Home Lending. It would take a year before all of the new loan originators and staff had moved into the same building, but essentially the deal was done. This was definitely a momentous milestone in Gold Star's relatively short history.

In late 2006, we held a client appreciation event in a local theater. It was an exciting day as loan officers who had previously been with three different companies gathered to thank our loyal customers. As I walked down the aisle to greet people and make a brief presentation, I remember thinking what a tremendous step this was. Almost overnight we had grown from 20 to 80 people and would now be recognized as an even bigger player on a regional and national scale. We would experience many other noteworthy developments during the next several years—launching more branch offices, hiring talented people from leading lenders, being publicly recognized as a business leader and thriving during the lending industry's meltdown. However, I knew I would always view this as a major turning point in Gold Star's development – and my own.

I have since had the opportunity to develop a company that has become a leader in the lending industry, while personally helping more than 30,000 customers realize their home ownership dreams. I have been asked to speak to various colleges and universities, financial institutions and other groups, and was appointed to the Board of Trustees at Cleary University. I have been recognized as one of the country's top originators for the last 10 years. It has been very fulfilling, considering my difficult start in the American business world. But I don't take anything for granted. I remember the long hours, the sleepless nights spent working in my office, the failures and many lessons learned along the way.

While I am still in my early thirties, I am running a large company that I founded and then expanded during this country's difficult economic period. I want to share some of the strategies and experiences that have made me successful. My goal is to help others succeed, while avoiding a few of the obstacles that I encountered as a salesperson and a company owner.

PART TWO
CORE VALUES

Chapter Four
The Nine Commandments of Sales Success

"Sales are contingent upon the attitude of the salesman - not the attitude of the prospect."
~W. Clement Stone

"DAN, I'LL GIVE YOU $1 MILLION if you share the secrets that have helped make you a top producing salesman."

Actually, I've grown tired of waiting for that request with the million dollar offer included, so I've decided to share my "mysterious" sales secrets with you for the price of this book. From my first days as a loan originator, I began developing a list of what I consider to be the keys to becoming a successful salesperson. Most of us have sought the advice of more experienced salespeople and other professionals at one time or another in our careers. That's why we read books, listen to motivational tapes and attend conferences. However, I believe that many salespeople sometimes fail to follow the right route, looking for short cuts to achieving financial rewards. I've found that most successful salespeople are generous in sharing some of their proven strategies, while others carefully guard their secrets, concerned that competition will overtake them.

Of course, the first secret I'm going to share with you is that there are no "secrets." Most salespeople are aware of at least some of the answers, the steps they must take to succeed. There is a core group of "best practices" and assorted addenda which, when followed closely, usually result in success.

Following are my *Nine Commandments for Sales Greatness.*

- **Don't Leave Home without Your Passion**—Ever since my McDonald's job, I've been fascinated by a quote from founder Ray Kroc: "If you work just for the money, you'll never make it, but if you love what you're doing and you always put the customer first, success will be yours." You need to wake up in the morning and be excited about selling. There are several motivating factors that inspire people to have a passion for sales: the challenge, pride in doing a good job, being recognized in a group of top sales professionals, and of course, the potential income. However, ultimately you simply must enjoy the process of selling a product or service. The old adage "enjoy your job and you will never work a day in your life," is absolutely true. Early in my career there were some days when I didn't want to work, and instead of pushing through those tough days, I made excuses. I had misplaced my passion for selling. However, I worked to regain that passion and never lost it again. The last time I called in sick was 12 years ago. I love what I do every day. Certainly there are days that are frustrating or difficult, but I would not trade a single one of those days for another career. Being a salesman is my passion and it has to be yours as well if you want to have a successful sales career.

  Whenever I talk with someone interested in the sales profession, I suggest they ask themselves to decide which of the following categories best describes their attitude: 1). I truly love selling and can't imagine doing anything else; 2). This is a job I'm pretty good at, but I can see myself doing other things; or 3). I find sales to be too challenging...I'm not sure if I'll ever be a real success at it. I explain that if they fall into the first category, they are already well on their way to a successful career. However, if they find themselves in the second or third category, a sales career might not be their best choice.

- **Be a Cheerleader For Your Product/Service**—You have to believe in what you're selling. Truly successful salespeople aren't just earning a commission or closing a deal; they are helping their clients in a measurable way, finding their first home, obtaining better terms on their current mortgage, delivering an insurance policy for a family's security or helping plan for the financial well-being of a newly-married couple. I've often said that "I'm the delivery boy for the American Dream of home ownership," anxious to help borrowers realize their important goals. They can see my enthusiasm, and know that I truly believe in the service I'm providing. As a salesman, you must believe in your product, otherwise clients will "see through you" and not buy.

Leading up to the mortgage industry meltdown, there were several toxic loan programs, such as subprime loans, negative amortization loans, and the so-called "liar loans" in which borrowers would not have to provide proof of income. All of these products turned out to be detrimental to borrowers and our economy – I did not believe in them, and I refused to sell them. Eventually, once I explained the programs and what they entailed, the borrowers would come around to my way of thinking. For instance, there was a customer for whom I had done several loans who called me to obtain a negative amortization loan at a one percent interest rate. I explained I didn't think it was a wise choice because of the problems others had experienced with this type of mortgage, resulting from an increase in the monthly adjustable interest rate and in the principal balance. However, he was adamant and when I couldn't dissuade him, he went to another lender. Two years later, the customer called to say he was sorry he had not listened to my advice. The one percent interest rate loan had not turned out well for him and he wanted my help in solving the situation. Unfortunately, I wasn't able to rescue him because he had been making minimum payments, was upside down with his loan and eventually lost the home to foreclosure.

Of course, there were many originators who did not believe in the potentially harmful loan programs' benefits but tried to sell them anyway. It is difficult to persuade someone about a product or service if you are not convinced yourself. Salespeople in other professions face similar situations. If you don't believe your company's product/service is beneficial to consumers, you should consider moving to a company or industry that has a product in which you do believe. Essentially, if you don't believe in apples, then sell oranges.

- **Make it About the Customer**—There is nothing more important than taking care of your customers. All salespeople know this essential fact: make one person unhappy and they'll soon tell 10 or more of their friends and associates about their unpleasant experience. If you upset a customer and aren't able to rectify the situation, it does not matter how much advertising you do because the damage has been done. It can take years to build trust with a customer, but only seconds to break it. It is nearly impossible to overcome a negative impression. The message here is *do everything possible to make your customers consider working with you as being one of the best decisions they ever made.* While writing this book, I received a call from a customer who wanted to complain about his closing costs being $750 more than he had originally anticipated. He opened the conversation by saying how much he disliked Gold Star and everyone associated with the lending business. Of course, he waited until seven months after the loan closing to complain, but that is beside the point. I asked the customer to hold while I checked his file. I said, "Sir, I do apologize for your bad experience. While I was not privy to your conversation with my loan officer, I want to make sure that all of my clients are satisfied."

"How do you plan on fixing it?" he asked.

I offered to refinance his home at no cost and with a rate of about 0.75% less than what his original purchase transaction was several months earlier. His tone immediately changed to "You're my family's savior Mr. Milstein." Of course, the moral of this story is that I kept the customer's satisfaction in the forefront of my mind. Instead of telling him that he had agreed to the fees and there was nothing I could do, I was able to save him about $40,000 on the life of his loan. Rather than merely paying the borrower $750 to go away, we kept a client and all of his future referrals while earning a $5,000 commission. In addition, before the new loan had even closed, he referred two of his co-workers to me. I was able to convert a problem into a "win-win" situation.

Customers come back to do business with me because I make them feel they are the most important people in the world. I take an interest in their lives, and ask about their families, their jobs and other areas of interest. Every time we speak, I try to imagine I am "walking in their shoes," because it gives me a better understanding of their situation.

It's essential that salespeople have the leeway to serve their customers the way they feel is best. One of our originators worked for a previous lender, whose sales manager didn't want her to pursue a customer with a small mortgage—a $20,000 loan at 9%. The customer was thrilled that she could lower her rate, explaining that several companies weren't interested because the loan was too small. However, the sales manager realized the salesperson was assisting with the loan and told her not to bother with it. The originator's response was that "everyone is entitled to save some money," and "I don't discriminate on the basis of loan amounts." After she had closed on the loan, the originator received a call from the borrower's sister who said she was told to call because of how grateful her family member was. It turned out the sister was a home builder and wanted help financing a subdivision of 60 homes. "My father taught me long ago to treat everyone equally and that what goes around comes around," the originator said.

- **Plan for a Crisis (and everything else)**—All salespeople must have short- and long-term plans. I'm not talking about a few goals written on a scrap of paper, but rather a formal plan that outlines target audiences, goals, strategies and measurement techniques. Of course, it starts with establishing basic goals. In a study done at Harvard University more than 40 years ago, researchers polled the graduating class of 1953 to find out how many students actually had clearly written specific goals and a plan for achieving them.

WHAT IT TAKES – WORDS OF WISDOM FROM SUCCESSFUL SALESPEOPLE

"In sales like in life: Work hard. Pay the price. There are no shortcuts in life. The jails are filled with people who thought otherwise."

—Alex Storozhenko, Merrill Lynch

"Attitude is everything. If you choose the negative attitude path, your path will certainly be rocky and largely unsuccessful."

"Be a student of the game. Endlessly grow your industry and sales acumen."

"Look within rather than blame others to foster sales attributes to the next level. Mirrors are everywhere."

"Do what you love. If you don't have love for what you do, your level of success will provide a panoramic image. Do you like your image?"

—Ryan Goodemoot, Gold Star

"Apply the FORD rule with every client: F = family, O = occupation, R = recreation (what they do in their spare time) and D = desire (what are their long term goals).

"Always tell the truth. You might lose sales short-term, but will get more business long-term.

"Don't appear desperate. Be prepared to lose deals; the salesperson is in control of transaction, not the client."

—Timothy Barry, Gold Star

"Always take the opportunity to keep your mouth shut. Listening is the number one skill that closes the deal each and every time."

—Alex Milshteyn, Edward Surovell Realtors

They were surprised to discover that in this class of highly intelligent people attending one of the world's most prestigious universities, only three percent had taken the time to write their goals. Even more significant, about 20 years later, when researchers checked back to see how the same group of graduates was doing, it seems that the three percent of the students who had written down their goals had accumulated more wealth than the other 97 percent of their class combined. They also found that these people seemed healthier and happier than their classmates.

You need to monitor your plans, goals and strategies regularly and make the appropriate modifications as the situation changes or your target audiences expand. For example, when I started out, I focused on emerging markets. However, that now accounts for less than five percent of my business. My target audience changed and I needed to adapt my marketing plan accordingly. You should also include a five and 10-year planning component. I never thought our company would be this size, so I've updated our 10-year plan several times. In today's more volatile market environment, you have to be more nimble, able to continually adapt your plan to meet new opportunities and obstacles. You also need to plan for contingencies, and a disaster preparedness plan is essential. For example, what will you do if the market collapses or if there is a slump in your own industry? You need to look beyond next month's or next year's income and determine the best route to long-term success during both "good and bad" market conditions.

- **Look Beyond Your Own Back Yard**—Too many salespeople give themselves restrictive boundaries. They don't look beyond their back yards, their designated market. Once you have conquered your town, move on to the next town. When you have the whole city covered, expand into the next one, and then the entire county, and when you're ready—the next state. When it was clear we wouldn't be able to achieve our long-term growth goals unless Gold Star was able to originate loans beyond Michigan's borders, we became licensed in more than 20 states. We took the company from a primarily regional to a national focus, which helped ensure we would succeed long-term. In Michigan alone, more than 90 percent of the mortgage lending companies closed during the well known "mortgage industry meltdown."

WHAT IT TAKES – WORDS OF WISDOM FROM SUCCESSFUL SALESPEOPLE
PART TWO

"Be an expert at what you are selling/providing, be it mortgages, or anything else. Do not ever be afraid of telling a client that you will have to get back to them on a detail that you want to confirm for them. Get the correct info quick, prove that you know what you are doing and have the resources to back it up.

"Provide way better service than the next guy.

"Be excited about what you do every time you come in contact with a client or potential client."

—Chris Sobszak, Gold Star

"If you're not taking care of your customer, your competition will.

"Always ask for the business and follow up. Never allow someone to be your priority while allowing yourself to be their option."

—Beth Larson, Jefferson Bank

*"I'm known for harping on many things, but if you ask any of my folks, I pound them on one simple principle that I am convinced if they do not do they will **not** be successful: **"HAVE A PLAN."** That means not just an "annual business plan," but a daily plan, a weekly plan, and a monthly plan. They should all tie directly into the salesperson's goals and objectives.*

—Rich Hoffmann, Flagstar Bank

An inability or unwillingness to diversify or otherwise expand their market was one of the reasons for their demise. Certainly there are many occasions where you will be assigned a certain geographic territory, but you can still expand in other ways. For example, when we first opened the Golden Rule office in Ann Arbor, we generated additional income by selling parking spaces at University of Michigan football games. I subsequently developed market niches with pro athletes. All salespeople have specific niche opportunities, such as seniors, immigrants, teachers, military personnel, and many others. In addition, we take full advantage of social media strategies, such as Facebook, LinkedIn and Twitter.

- **Answer Your Phone; Be There**— Selling isn't a 9:00 to 5:00 job and this is especially true when you're starting out. It can be an all-encompassing job where you must be available 24 hours a day, seven days a week, 365 days a year, especially if you are selling to clients on a national scale. You need to be accessible. I have a framed napkin in my office that illustrates the value we place on accessibility. It's a reminder of an event that occurred late at night after we had enjoyed an evening out at a restaurant to review the week's successes. It was about 2:15 a.m. when my phone rang; it was a transfer from my sales line. I answered and obviously surprised the Dallas-based airline pilot who had just landed after an overseas flight and intended to leave a message about his desired loan. He was shocked that someone picked up. However, I told him I had plenty of time to help and proceeded to use a cocktail napkin to take an application for a $450,000 loan with 20 percent down. I thanked the pilot and said I would get him a rate quote as soon as the market opened. After our conversation, I turned to my associates and said. "Do you think he would have called someone else after leaving a message with us?" He certainly would have. But since I answered the phone and impressed him with my dedication, I had made a lifetime client. We worked to get his home financing completed in a timely fashion and closed without any hitches. Pilots frequently move so they can be great referral sources. To date, this pilot has recommended at least seven clients to me, who also have referred their friends. The "ball has continued to bounce" because we were available late at night and had a 15 minute phone conversation.

In another instance, a celebrity photographer called from his hotel room in Florida. He, his wife and newborn child were stuck in a hotel room because his current lender was unable to close their loan as promised. I took his call at 9:00 p.m. on Friday, while most people in the industry were relaxing after another long week. I called in my support team over the weekend and we used all of our resources to close this loan on Monday, less than 72 hours after he called. Ever since, this customer has sent me many of his supermodel and celebrity clients, as well as family members from throughout the country. Had I not been available right then, he probably would have gone somewhere else.

WHAT IT TAKES – WORDS OF WISDOM FROM SUCCESSFUL SALESPEOPLE
ONE MORE

Overcome Objections—*The sale actually begins when the customer says "no." The best salespeople are able to overcome customers' objections. Smart consumers are often the hardest to sell. They have generally done their research beforehand. Some are determined to prove to you that they aren't a pushover. These customers will have a litany of objections in order to drive down the price of whatever they happen to be buying. You've heard most of them before: "It's too expensive," and "It doesn't seem like the right program (mortgage, insurance, stock, etc.)," or a favorite one—"I'm just not ready right now." The latter is especially curious when stated by those who called to ask you for a quote. You must be prepared to handle these objections without stumbling. If you just ramble on about irrelevant topics and belabor your initial sales pitch, you're not convincing anybody. You must be prepared to respond to any objections clearly and concisely, explain why it is still in the customer's best interests to purchase your product and then try to close the deal.*

High accessibility is the key component of business relationships with both customers and your strategic referral partners, such as attorneys, CPAs, financial planners and others. Very few people have the ability to leave work early or step away from their office to attend several daily appointments. Indeed, being available to clients in the evening and on weekends shows your utmost commitment to them and their needs. I have yet to meet a Realtor who has failed to inquire about my availability in the evening, and on weekends and holidays. This level of accessibility is important to real estate agents, as they often show homes to clients in the evenings and on weekends. When a client is ready to make an offer on a home and has financing questions, they need prompt answers. Having a loan officer who is constantly available to explain the process, terms, and conditions in a manner that is easily understandable is paramount to a successful business relationship. While it may not be necessary for salespeople in other professions to be similarly available, there are other ways to demonstrate your accessibility. This may involve providing your e-mail address or "after hours" cell number so that a customer can contact you with a question and know that she will receive a prompt response.

- Market Yourself Creatively—"Word of mouth," relying on your past customers to tell others how great you are, just isn't enough. The sales profession is too competitive to think that you can make it without promoting yourself. Salespeople spend billions of dollars developing sophisticated marketing campaigns, including a mix of direct mail, advertising, co-op marketing with strategic partners, newsletters, social media, and many other strategies. Early on, you should establish a personal marketing program, one that sets you apart from your competitors. You must let the world know that you exist and that you are different and better than the competition. The world does not beat a path to the door of the best clockmaker and demand his products. Rather, it is up to the clockmaker to let the world know that he exists.

When the market gets a little sluggish, don't stop marketing. That's what a lot of your competitors do; somehow believing that it is wise to reduce marketing-related expenditures, which can quickly slow the momentum of a strong promotional campaign. I remember hearing the simple anecdote about a hot dog salesman that illustrates the need to continue marketing during difficult economic conditions. It is the story of a hardworking man who lacked formal training in business or any other traditional skill. He thought he might be good at sales and started out on a small scale, with a hot dog stand on the corner of a busy street. At first, he didn't do much marketing, other than yell "Get your hot dogs here." But people liked his hot dogs and the business slowly grew. He cautiously expanded the tiny operation, adding a larger grill and a colorful sign above the stand. Then he began posting fliers at neighboring shops. The hot dog business became so successful that he was able to begin saving money and even cover the costs of his son's college education. Several years later, his son graduated with a marketing degree and returned home. The young man was appreciative of what his father had done, but also wanted to share his vast knowledge of how to run a business during what was then a recession. "I think you need to revamp the business and cut back on your marketing costs," he advised his dad. The hot dog entrepreneur was worried about the future and believing his son was right, began to make changes. He stopped posting fliers, dropped plans to advertise in the local business publication and reduced the number of hot dogs on his menu. One evening, he walked in the house with a sad look on his face. When the son asked what had happened, the previously successful salesman replied, "You were right, the recession has really slowed sales. It's tougher than ever out there." Of course, the son shouldn't have meddled with his father's basic, but effective sales strategy. The next time you face a business slump within your own industry, consider the value of maintaining your marketing campaign and even increase it slightly to stand apart from the competition.

- **Be Positive...or Else**—Believe me, there's no seat at the table for complainers. Sales managers, customers and most everyone else hate to be around crybabies. When salespeople whine about high interest rates, lack of loan or insurance programs, the commission structure, pricing policies or an array of other issues, they are often looking to rationalize their own shortcomings rather than find solutions. It leaves a negative impression on those around them, and can eventually cost them customers who wish to be associated with a more positive environment.

A poor attitude can even cost you your job if it affects the rest of your team. Consider the story about the sales manager who witnessed the "complaining rash" spreading throughout his office. He recalled that everybody decided to collectively gripe to management about poor interest rates, processing issues and other problems. As he said, "Those who aren't selling, spend a lot of time talking about how bad rates are, how bad service is and pretty much anything else to give them an excuse for their lack of production. When you're out there pounding the pavement, your focus is selling and therefore rates and service fall out of your chief areas of concern." The manager's response to the complainers was simple and straightforward: "If it's bad where you are, go somewhere else. If it's bad everywhere, sell something else. If everything you sell is bad, then go drive a bus, because you aren't a salesman." Everyone has occasional off days when production is not as high as it could be. Perhaps personal issues are interfering and making work seem intolerable. Perhaps your production is sluggish because of the difficult economy. I am the first to admit that selling a loan at 4% is a lot easier than selling a loan when rates are 6%. Extraneous factors come into play and everyone knows there are bad days. However, a positive attitude—about your company and its products, customers, vendors and fellow employees—is critical for success.

Charles Swindoll, the writer and clergyman, had a great philosophy on the importance of having the right attitude. He emphasized that maintaining a positive outlook is critical to the well-being of individuals, families, companies and society in general. Swindoll explained that this is more important than an education, wealth, talent, and just about everything else. He pointed out that it's up to us to start each day with the right attitude and that it is certainly within our power to do so. While he wasn't talking specifically about salespeople, there is an obvious connection. If we embrace an upbeat attitude, it's inevitable we will gain more personal satisfaction and sales success throughout the day.

• Take a risk, be bold—You've got to be courageous, take a stand when it might be difficult to do so. This may involve creating a special campaign, offering a service that no one else has, cutting ties with non-productive referral partners, reducing your fees or taking some other action that salespeople at your office or elsewhere might not be willing to do. Look ahead to what you feel will help establish yourself as a "winner" among your customers and prospects, and then take the necessary steps to get there. You may encounter obstacles along the way. I was comfortable at my first real job at McDonald's, but because I sought a new challenge, decided that the tire store job was worth the risk (and pay cut). I twice took a bold leap to become a mortgage broker and even though both times I didn't succeed, the experience was worth the risk. Later, I left the comfort (and significant income) of my underwriting job to open the Golden Rule office, then pushed myself to launch Gold Star. These were aggressive actions at the time. Gold Star has continued to take risks—from establishing new offices to offering new services—in order to enhance our national visibility, increase market share and of course, to ensure the loyalty of our valued customers.

Your actions may not have an immediate payoff, but remember that the most rewarding plans often don't lead to quick results. The goal is to be successful after others have left the market. The most successful business people—such as Bill Gates and Warren Buffet—have excelled by being willing to take risks.

So, here it is, the magic list of *secrets* you need to get started and enjoy your first level of success: be passionate about sales, believe in your product, take care of customers, plan ahead, be available, expand your presence, be a creative marketer, have a positive outlook and take risks.

Oh, and there is one more commandment I'd like you to obey:

—Always Be Closing.

Chapter Five
ABC - Always Be Closing

"Winners make a habit of manufacturing their own positive expectations in advance of the event."

~Brian Tracy

A NYONE WHO KNOWS ME well is probably shocked that in the last chapter I ignored the most important secret of sales success. They will be happy to learn that the 10th commandment—*Always Be Closing*—is getting a separate chapter. In fact, this mantra is the main thing I had in mind for the "ABC" in the title of this book.

Many otherwise successful salespeople sometimes miss the fact that you have to take advantage of every sales opportunity. You cannot overlook anything. I have met some great sales prospects at fundraising dinners, on airplanes, right before a crucial play in a college football game – even walking on a beach in Miami.

Rick Richter and I were taking a quick break during a business trip to Miami. It was a beautiful day and we were walking along the shore when we heard a nearby couple tell their hotel's outdoor waiter to charge their drinks to an unusual name. I turned to them and casually asked if they knew a client of mine who shared the same last name. In one of those amazing "this is a small world" coincidences, it turned out that they did; the man relaxing on the beach was the brother of my client, a Detroit-area judge for whom I had previously arranged a purchase loan.

Not wanting to pass up a potential new client, I began a casual conversation about various topics, including the couple's home state of Georgia, their relative and his family, and the pleasant Miami weather. Eventually, the conversation switched to our professions. "I am your 'go-to' mortgage guy if you need home financing," I cheerfully told the couple. That seemed to interest my new acquaintances, who proceeded to ask me about the market and housing situation. I shared my insights about the market trends and where interest rates were headed. One topic led to another and it wasn't long before I had the start of a loan application written on a cocktail napkin, and another loyal customer. As Rick and I continued walking down the beach, I smiled and said, "ABC."

Seizing The Opportunities

ABC—*Always Be Closing is* one of my favorite phrases, a motto that I live by and one of the prime reasons I have been successful as a salesman. I never turn off my selling mindset. I'm always ready to engage a friend, colleague, or stranger in conversations that will lead to a sale. I am especially interested in pursuing the unexpected sales opportunities, the type that some overlook and the more enterprising salespeople embrace. This is not to say that I'm the only salesperson who would have taken advantage of that sales opportunity in Miami, but many others would have let the beach atmosphere interfere with their sales radar.

On another occasion, I was at a Detroit Red Wings game when I overheard a nearby seatmate talk about the interest rates and the difficulty her cousin had in finding a mortgage. What an easy opening! "I currently have five clients (hockey players) skating out there on the ice, and I advise your cousin to use the best to help with her mortgage," I said. At a different game I casually announced, "That is my client (a premier hockey player) who just scored." Of course, it prompted a few people to ask: "What do you do?" That was my cue for a brief sales introduction.

One of our salespeople experienced an impromptu opportunity at his daughter's ballet recital. Tim naturally applauded loudly at his young ballerina's performance, and then joined other parents who gathered in the lobby for a brief intermission. As he stood in line for a soda, he began talking to another father. "Amazing what they have done, isn't it?" Tim commented. "Absolutely," the other father commented. "I can't believe they can twirl around like that and never lose their balance." Tim said that it reminded him of how he felt when he was in his office, moving back and forth among papers and files while on the phone with a client. "That sounds like a tough job," the other father remarked and then asked the all-important question. "So, what do you do for a living?" Tim had a receptive audience as he explained his profession. Within a few days, he was refinancing his new acquaintance's home and eventually handled loans for 10 of the man's friends and neighbors, all because he had realized the potential of a brief encounter at his daughter's recital.

I have found divorce attorneys and policemen to be especially receptive to these "impromptu" selling possibilities:

- During divorce proceedings involving two of our employees, I was asked to provide a deposition. After detailing my professional responsibilities, I offered the appropriate information regarding the employees' status. When the interview was over, I had a chance to talk with the attorneys for a few minutes and I answered questions regarding the challenging lending market. The wife's attorney obviously did her homework; the following day she called to ask for help with a refinance.

- A police officer stopped a Gold Star loan originator who was speeding on his way to an evening client meeting. The policeman seemed to be interested that he was a mortgage loan officer. After exchanging his business card for the ticket, our originator drove a little slower to his customer meeting. The next morning he received a phone call from the policeman who was looking for a good deal on his new mortgage.

- Another policeman came to our headquarters looking for a young woman who had briefly worked as a temp employee at Gold Star. It seems she had missed her court appearance to testify in an accident case. I told the officer I would be glad to help him track down the errant witness and invited him to my office. After trying to reach the former employee at her home, we briefly discussed various topics, including of course, home financing and current interest rates. Before he left that day, one of Michigan's finest provided enough pertinent details to get his own loan application started.

There have been numerous times I have been at a dinner gathering or cocktail party when one of the guests commented "I'm not sure if it really is a good time to refinance," or "I've heard some good and bad things about reverse mortgages...you just don't know who to trust," or "I've been renting so long, it seems so difficult to get a home loan these days..." Within seconds I responded that I was in the mortgage business and would welcome the opportunity to help. I have received many morning calls starting with, "We met last night and you suggested I contact you."

Of course, I enjoy discussing topics other than home finance; three of my favorite subjects are sports, history and politics. Yet, I am always primed for a sales opportunity. I have met a few other salespeople who have the same instincts. No matter what product or service you are selling, just think of the sales potential. Many salespeople avoid "selling" when they are in social settings such as a neighborhood party, football tailgate gathering or other event. It seems they do not like being in a business mode 24/7. I always felt that these are some of the best times to make sales. You are already ahead of "the pack" because you are dealing with people in a friendly manner as opposed to in an office. The prospects have invited you to help them and are just waiting for you to provide answers to their specific needs.

Certainly there are limitations to the *Always Be Closing* approach. I was at a funeral for a business acquaintance and afterwards was speaking to a few people. I was surprised to overhear a man talking to the wife of the deceased. He was a Realtor who explained that he was quite successful and could help her sell the family house. It wasn't the best time to make such an arrangement. Most savvy salespeople know when to refrain from talking business at such inopportune occasions.

ABC Selling Skills

The most successful salespeople have mastered a special set of skills that are important in all selling, but particularly relevant in the more spontaneous situations. Although this is now something I do automatically, there are a series of key disciplines that I developed over a period of several years. They include:

Communicate Effectively

Most important, you have to connect with your prospects by being outgoing, personable and confident. Some salespeople are reserved and unsure. They are knowledgeable and committed to their customers but somewhat uncomfortable in social situations, making it difficult to react to the more spontaneous sales opportunities. Others are self-assured and personable; they are comfortable speaking with new people and extremely confident in their abilities, but not pushy. Still others are overly aggressive and often make listeners uncomfortable. Obviously, you want to be in the second group, although it may take practice to find your comfort zone.

People who thrive in social settings are able to connect with others and make each individual feel like the most important person in the room. Corporate consultant Nicholas Boothman has noted that all meetings and interactions offer unique opportunities and learning how to take advantage of them is critical to business success. How do you become the confident salesperson who relates well to prospective customers in diverse situations? Certainly there is no singular approach; however here are some guidelines that we encourage our originator trainees and others to follow:

- Look people in the eye and smile—Eye contact is essential to convey trust and a sincere smile helps establish instant rapport with your audience.

- Pay attention to body language—There are many theories on how body language impacts your listener's response. The key is to look comfortable; avoid folding your arms and leaning too far forward.

- Be interested—You want to show genuine interest in your audience. Ask questions about their profession and personal life, use their name, and solicit their feedback.

- **State Your Case**—While you want to allow the prospect to have center stage and talk about themselves, you want to make them aware of what you do and how you can help. In addition, I have found that salespeople are generally more confident when they know they can offer customers the best possible deal. Advising prospects that they should "Call other stores and you will find that we have the best price available on that model," will help to instill confidence that you are the right person for them to be talking to. Most people won't contact other competitors; it is enough that you are reassuring them your fees are the most reasonable available. Of course, you need to be certain that your best price pledge is valid. Never make a promise that you are unable to keep.

Listen for Signals

Perhaps the most critical ABC ability is being an exceptionally good listener so that you don't overlook potential sales opportunities. You must be able to follow multiple conversations, to pick up on such phrases as "tired of renting," "life insurance is too expensive," "Does the Realtor work for the seller or the buyer? "Will the market ever get better?" and so on. This doesn't mean that you have to hover near groups of people at a party or eavesdrop on conversations. You just need to keep yourself attuned to the appropriate signs.

Perfect Your Elevator Speech

Picture this: you are on a crowded elevator. Several people are discussing the day's events, how much they love or hate their job and their plans for the weekend. The man next to you sees your armload of files and asks, "So what do you do?" You're only traveling a few floors and feel you couldn't possibly explain your profession in such a short time so you say, "I am in sales." Perhaps that ends the conversation.

Or, you can share something a little more informative, such as "I'm a mortgage banker, always interested in helping first-time borrowers and anyone else wanting to purchase or refinance a home. With rates at current lows, this is an ideal time. And news reports to the contrary, it really doesn't take forever to close these days. So if you know of anyone interested, have them call me." Or,

"I heard you mention your frustration at finding the right life insurance program. I agree that it can be a little complicated, but it doesn't have to be if you do your homework. Perhaps I can help; I am an insurance broker representing more than 25 different companies. Based on your specific needs and other variables, I can assist you in finding the right one."

In other words, you should be prepared to succinctly explain what you do in about the 30 seconds it might take to reach your prospect's floor. The elevator speech is a great ABC tool, and if you don't have one, you need to prepare it right away. Just make sure that your elevator speech is not too complicated or "scripted." Practice until you are sure it sounds conversational.

Watch the Clock

When someone says, "I read an article about refinancing," or "Someone mentioned the benefits of term insurance," or whatever the topic, you have a brief window to make a valuable customer contact. You must have your 30 or 60 second message ready. If you hesitate, the conversation may quickly shift to another topic and you might find it awkward to return to mortgages, insurance, real estate or whatever you sell.

Time limits are more generally critical than you might think in these situations. If you turn your elevator speech into a half-hour sermon, you will likely bore your audience, squander the opportunity to make a sale and possibly not be invited to the next neighborhood party. Certainly there is a certain "conversation line" you don't cross, although it will vary depending on the situation. If you notice a clear-cut sign of boredom or frustration—the other person is shifting in his seat, gazing around the room or trying to change the subject—it is definitely time to conclude your message. The bottom line is that you do not want to impose your sales will on people, but it is fine to be polite about your business without being overbearing. I am never obnoxious in my conversations. I have learned through experience just the right information to share without losing my audience.

Consider the Passive Approach

There is also the more passive, yet effective selling technique. For example, as my Gold Star colleagues will attest, I'm frequently on one of my cell phones—talking to customers or prospects. A bystander might hear my conversation and later ask about my profession, thus providing a chance for me to explain how I can help them. A few years ago, I was flying with a few friends to a hockey game in another state. I was on the phone with a client, enthusiastically explaining how we were going to close his loan in a few days. The co-pilot overheard the discussion and when we landed he said, "So you're in the mortgage business…" and we proceeded to discuss his needs for home financing. I have been in similar situations at airports, in movie

---

THE MENTOR'S ROLE

Dan taught me everything I know, he excelled as a mentor. I would take sales calls, and you could hear him from the office walls coaching me on what to say. At first I found it annoying and distracting, but I gradually saw the benefit of his armchair assistance. It was as if he was listening to the conversation on the other end. It was sort of comical to people walking around in the office hearing him shout to me about new financial news to throw into my pitch, or saying that certain fees couldn't be controlled. He knew everything a certain prospect would say. He knew their personality within 30 seconds of being on the phone and how he would sell them a loan. The type of person on either side of the phone could be the most difficult sale in the world, but Dan would make it look easy.

—Chris Wilson, a Gold Star Mortgage loan officer

---

theater lines, the grocery store and the doctor's office. Some salespeople use other incentives to generate discussion and sales opportunities. For example, I know of a loan originator who wore an "Ask Me How I can Save You Money on Your Next Home Loan" badge while he walked through a professional football game tailgate gathering. It had the desired effect. This experienced salesman was stopped several times by people who asked him how he would be able to help them save on their future home purchase or refinance.

He made a lot of great contacts that afternoon and most likely obtained a few new clients as well. I have seen other salespeople do something similar at community events, creating interest among potential customers who might be ready to purchase a car, home, wide screen television, insurance policy or living room furniture.

Cross Selling

All salespeople should be skilled at cross selling, whereby they follow up their initial discussion with a mention of another product or service, as a way to expand their sales options. Of course, financial institutions typically have a variety of products, including savings and checking accounts, consumer and home loans, and credit lines. Insurance salespeople have similar options, able to offer their prospects life, disability, medical and other coverage. Even salespeople with more limited product menus can offer ancillary products or services, including accessories and extended warranties.

You can take advantage of a prospect's initial interest by sharing information on related products, stressing how they can help achieve short and long-term goals. It is easy to make an appropriate shift. For example: "Now that you are all set with life insurance, you might have an interest in some cost effective medical and homeowners' programs…"

Don't Forget the Close

The first part of ABC focuses on the sales function, the importance of continually taking advantage of chances to sell your service or product at sporting activities, social occasions, fundraising events and every other conceivable situation. Once you have the customer engaged and potentially ready to purchase, you have to take that last, critical step. You have gained an opportunity to sell your product or service, now you have to be able to close the sale. Obviously, closing is a greater challenge when dealing with prospects who aren't yet convinced they need the product or are still shopping other firms. The close is much easier when you are talking to a referral or someone else who is already primed to purchase from you.

In my first two mortgage broker positions, I lacked the requisite knowledge about interest rate locks and other aspects of the closing process. I was passionate about sales, but didn't have a sufficient understanding of the basics to convince borrowers to purchase right then. Once I was more knowledgeable and also had more backroom support and the ability to provide customers with specific solutions for their purchase or refinance, my closing rate increased dramatically.

There are many salespeople who are extremely knowledgeable about their particular industry, have a strong work ethic and appear to be quite successful, yet don't reach their potential because they fail to achieve the most important goal; a high closing rate. This deficiency can prevent even the most determined salesperson from succeeding. I know a financial services advisor who often visits a restaurant frequented by a variety of professionals; the type the financial planner would certainly like to have as clients. He is friendly and a great talker. In fact, he occasionally spends a few minutes behind the grill assisting the cooks or socializing in the bar. Everyone seems to like him. However, I learned that the majority of these prospects aren't especially interested in investing in his firm's programs. This could be for a variety of reasons. Perhaps people think he is "nice," but not especially knowledgeable. Whatever the reason, he isn't closing.

Salespeople often cite a myriad of excuses for their inability to close: "The prospect just isn't ready to buy," "It wasn't a good lead," "The competition has a better deal," or, "It's winter and people aren't leaving their houses to shop."

Whatever the excuse, this salesperson is unable or unwilling to take advantage of the momentum already established in previous discussions with qualified prospects (not those who are merely "testing the waters" regarding a product or service). He may come within an inch of closing, but ultimately let the sale stall with the hope that he will make it happen the next day. However, by that time the prospect may have talked to another salesperson or put the transaction on the "back burner." You can strengthen your closing expertise by:

- **Answering Objections**—All salespeople encounter objections or other potential closing delays that are often imposed by the prospect. I have talked with many salespeople who are adept at most areas, but have a marginal ability to effectively handle objections. The key is to develop a list of the most frequent customer objections that your customers have made and be certain that you are able to answer them convincingly. The ability to answer objections to the client's satisfaction can make the difference between a timely close and no close.

---

5 KEYS TO EFFECTIVE CLOSINGS

1. *Put yourself in the customer's shoes, anticipating their needs.*

2. *Listen carefully to customers discuss their concerns. Buyers frequently "close themselves," by reviewing their situation and concluding they have made a wise decision. Avoid talking so much that you inadvertently create new closing obstacles.*

3. *Answer each of their objections.*

4. *Restate your solution: "So Helen, as agreed, this (product/service) will help you realize your goals by_____. You have made a good choice."*

5. *Request the action. ("Let's start your application now," or "I will have all of the paperwork ready for you; let's meet tomorrow at xxx.")*

- **Confirming Their Needs**—As you approach the end of a sales call or presentation, you may think you have answered all of the prospect's questions or concerns. However, there still may be some uncertainty about the price, product guarantee, delivery date or other important details. The best way to be certain there are no remaining issues is to verify with the customer. For instance, if you believe the prospect has any final reservations, just say "Mr. Jones, what would it take to gain your business today?" or "What else can I do to help you make a decision today?" At this point, they typically will suggest any remaining questions and allow you to move forward to the final step.

- Asking for the Business—Some salespeople have difficulty closing the sale because they miss one final element: asking for the business. They already have provided the necessary information, offered solutions to the customer's situation and answered the primary objections, yet not made the final move. They inadvertently let the customer take control of the situation by stalling. "Let me think about it for a couple of days," or "It all sounds good, but I don't know…" are two common customer responses. It may be as simple as advising the prospect, "Why don't we proceed and complete the application," or "Let's sit down and write up the contract for your new computer system." Prospects often just need a slight encouragement to get them to act.

Analyzing Your ABC Skills

If you are not meeting your self-imposed or company mandated closing goals, you need to examine the causes and make the necessary modifications. First, measure your closing ratio. How many real sales calls did you make last month or year? These aren't the casual conversations you have had with people, but rather those instances where you have actually been in a position to sell. How many resulted in closed sales? If you haven't been keeping track of this important statistic, begin doing so now.

Then analyze what is preventing you from closing more sales. While salespeople often attribute their lack of success to a company deficiency—such as higher prices or slow turnaround—your long-term success as a closer is ultimately your responsibility. Perhaps you aren't able to satisfactorily address the prospects' questions or objections. Or you simply have not asked for the business. Objectively examine your last 10 failed (or delayed) closings to see if you can identify the problem.

To help refine your sales and closing expertise, you can enlist the support of a more experienced salesperson who is willing to critique your strategies. Have them listen to several of your phone calls and sit in on customer meetings and then offer suggestions for improvement. You can also tape your own calls to replay later (you are required by law to let the person at the other end of the line know that you are taping the conversation). Salespeople may think they have had an ideal conversation with a prospect, only to realize later that they talked too fast, monopolized the conversation or didn't adequately answer the prospect's questions. By studying your presentation, you should be able to pinpoint any mistakes and make the appropriate adjustments, which can include adhering to the previous guidelines.

We spend a great deal of time helping our salespeople polish their closing strategies. Gold Star has an informal "closing academy" that includes reviewing telephone scripts, monitoring conversations and adjusting originators' conversation styles. We listen to their prospect calls and offer suggestions about their initial approach and how they handle the close. While we don't have an actual graduation exercise, these "students" know that their class in *The ABC of Sales* will help ensure a long and successful career.

I always tell salespeople looking for an edge against their competition to be attuned to the unusual and unexpected sales opportunities. "It doesn't take that much more effort to get in the Always Be Closing mindset," I remind them. "After a while, it becomes second nature. And you will find that your day, and indeed your career, will be that much more exciting and rewarding."

Chapter Six
Listen to The Warden, and Paint the Porch

"A sale is not something you pursue; it's what happens to you while you are immersed in serving your customer."

~Unknown

OME SALESPEOPLE WILL DO almost anything to impress their customers – even go to prison.

There are two main reasons a loan originator would visit a dreary prison. The first is obvious; they have committed fraud. The less apparent reason would be to have an inmate sign documents to facilitate a loan transaction. Mike Hyman, one of our veteran originators, entered a bleak Michigan prison one winter afternoon several years ago with the latter purpose in mind, to help a previous customer avoid losing her house. The customer asked him to refinance her mortgage; she was struggling with her payments and had a high interest rate. Mike was able to put together a loan that would greatly reduce her payment with a low fixed-rate program. Everything was fine until he received the title work, which listed her ex-husband. Mike explained that her ex simply needed to sign a quitclaim deed (relinquishing his ownership rights), since the divorce papers specified that the house was hers alone. The customer assured him this was the case, but became very upset when he mentioned the deed. She finally explained that her ex-husband had just gone to prison, which was over eight hours away. The deed would have to be taken to him, because the prison warden said they could not just send the paperwork. When Mike learned his client was unable to drive her car, he promised to find a notary to visit the prison and get the form signed. Of course, she was ecstatic. This unusual transaction changed her life, as she might have been unable to refinance the house and end up losing it, if her ex-husband hadn't been removed from the title. The client continues to remember Mike with referrals.

Going The Extra Mile

The prison incident is an ideal example of salespeople making an extreme effort to satisfy their customers' often challenging situations. Most salespeople and sales managers exclaim that customer service is critically important, yet they focus solely on the basics, providing a good product at a reasonable cost in a timely manner. That is the traditional "common sense" business approach. They want to ensure a sufficiently high Return on Investment and balk when faced with unusual events that take too much time or cost a little extra to solve. They tend to forget that customers who get the excellent service they deserve will nearly always richly reward the salesperson with referrals.

GOLD STAR PLEDGE

We will do whatever is necessary to ensure our clients' needs are met and surpassed in a timely, friendly and ethical manner. We go out of our way to overcome all obstacles while satisfying (and often surprising) our valued customers as they seek to purchase or refinance a home.

Joe Girard, the legendary auto salesman, was one of the early proponents of exceptional customer service. For example, he knew that customers dislike waiting to have their cars overhauled, so he provided first class treatment. Girard would often instruct his mechanics to actually work on cars while the owners were waiting at the curb. He would later recall that after watching the mechanics install new parts and make other adjustments to their cars, customers would ask how much they owed. Girard always smiled and usually said there would be no charge. He explained that he appreciated his customers and wanted them to come back.

Girard didn't spend time over-analyzing the costs involved in providing his customers with this extraordinary curb-side service. He was committed to doing whatever was necessary to ensure that they were given the best possible care. He was acutely aware of the two reasons to go beyond the norm:

1. Customers deserve to be treated well. Remember the Golden Sales Rule: "Give your customers white glove service, just as you would wish to be treated."

2. People remember when a salesperson has provided exceptional service. They are more likely to become long-term clients.

Gail and Joe Owen were a significant influence in my own quest to master the art of customer service. Working for them I was able to hit my stride as a top-performing salesman, but looking back I was a "sales machine" who concentrated on the ABC of lending. I was not necessarily conversant in the nuances of customer service. I frequently visited Gail and Joe at their Tampa headquarters and was impressed with how they related to their customers. I listened to Gail speak to customers on a personal level, offering her insights and assistance on their family and other concerns. We spoke about the need to put the borrower's welfare above the loan originator's financial incentive. I was impressed with how she went out of her way to be more than a salesperson to her clients. By observing the Owens and a few other sales professionals I admired, I gained a better appreciation of the meaning of exceptional customer service.

During the last several years, we have developed and refined Gold Star's own customer service model, by researching, listening to clients and brainstorming with our salespeople. Of course, we take care of the basics: providing the best possible loan and rate, ongoing communications and fast turnaround. However, our goal is to go "above and beyond" to meet the special circumstances that a salesperson frequently encounters. For example, in order to ensure prompt customer follow-up, we eliminated the normal voice-mail system by giving our sales force an 800 number that is also connected to their cell phones. After the phone rings four times, it connects to the cell, thus minimizing response time.

We also developed the Gold Star Concierge program to further set us apart from other firms. As part of this special service, we provide customers with a prepaid 60-minute 800-number that enables them to call our concierge representative to receive assistance in a variety of ways: making travel arrangements, securing entertainment reservations, personal shopping and corporate research. This benefit has become extremely popular; customers don't expect personal attention like that from most companies. We continually encourage our salespeople to go beyond the norm when servicing their customers. Obviously, this same approach can be applied to any type of sales.

Offering High Level Service

There are many ways to show customers that you appreciate them. I had an opportunity to illustrate our customer-centric approach during a conference of mortgage professionals in Las Vegas. My colleague Rick Richter and I were asked to speak to the loan officers of a large mortgage company. There were about 300 loan officers staring attentively and ready to learn. Rick gave a presentation on how to ramp up your pipeline if you are new to the business. Then I began my talk about what it takes to be on the short list of the top 200 originators nationwide.

After about five minutes, I stopped, grabbed my BlackBerry and started to read an e-mail. The audience grew restless and some people seemed a little offended. I looked up, smiled and explained, "This is what it takes to be the best. You have to be ready to drop everything for your clients. If you're consistent with this, you will get a reputation for being available. Realtors and referral partners will know that when they call, you will be ready to assist them." I let them know I did that on purpose to prove a point. The group responded positively; it was clear they understood my message and by the end of the presentation, they were fired up and ready to take on the world.

THE EXTRA MEASURES

What salespeople will do to satisfy their customers.

"We were about to close on a customer's property, but underwriting stipulated we needed to correct the peeling paint that the appraiser noted on the porch. I anticipated new hand-wringing by my client, the seller and both agents regarding scheduling, cost and other issues. So, the next day I spent an hour painting the porch, then ordered the final inspection and closed the transaction."

"I drove to the home of a customer who was purchasing in the dead of winter and personally shoveled the snow off the roof in order to pass the FHA/home inspection and close the loan before year's end. (I brought a friend in case I fell.)"

"I once went out in the middle of January to help a borrower patch his driveway to meet an FHA repair condition."

— Successful Salespeople

There are many key aspects to enhanced customer service, including the following key points.

Addressing communication problems

Sometimes salespeople need to take extra measures when there has been inadvertent miscommunication that has created a problem. Perhaps a customer misunderstood the application requirements, timing, or other elements of the transaction. Here's an interesting and costly example that seems more humorous now than it did at the time. A 75 year-old client for whom I had arranged several previous loans wanted to purchase a $1 million house. We pre-approved him and waited for his response. When the customer didn't call back, I assumed he had decided against the purchase. Then a month later, he came to my office with two Realtors and the seller – for the closing! Of course, I was surprised and explained there was no closing scheduled, that in fact we had only pre-approved him. That's not what he, the agents or the seller wanted to hear, as he needed the money in order to close on his new house. They didn't want to leave my office until we had this settled. While it was the customer's misunderstanding, I realized I should have followed-up. I calculated the likely results if we simply told everyone we would have to wait until everything was arranged and a new closing was scheduled. Not willing to risk the negative reactions, I first offered to pay the seller $2,000 to cancel his moving expenses. I then called my community bank and opened a line of credit to enable me to provide the client with immediate financing for his house. He, the seller and agents were happy, and I was reminded of a very important "law of customer service": always make sure you and your customer are in agreement on all matters, and if there is a mistake, take care of it right away.

Protect customers' interests at all costs.

In 2003, interest rates were near an all-time low—about 4.875 percent for a 30-year fixed rate mortgage. However, they started creeping upwards to about 6.75 percent. Many mortgage originators, perhaps a little on the greedy side, were not overly concerned about locking in rates for their customers. Later they blamed others and the market conditions for not being able to secure rates for their customers' benefit. I realized it was important to protect my clients' interests and as a result, I paid more than $48,000 in rate lock extensions. Most people thought I was crazy. "Why are you doing that?" they would ask. "It's not as if those customers are coming back," one of my colleagues stressed. Yet my customers' welfare was of the utmost importance. Indeed, I felt my reputation was on the line. Perhaps it was a good business sense, along with "positive karma," but every one of those customers continued to do business with me. I delivered on what I promised, and made the $48,000 back many times over by later assisting them with refinances, investment home purchases, second mortgages and new homes, in addition to the second and third generation referrals that resulted.

Another example of helping protect clients' interests involved a veteran financial services advisor whose client is required to take a minimum distribution from his retirement accounts every year. Failing to take the money from the retirement account before December 31 can result in a severe IRS penalty, over $50,000 in this case.

EXTRA MEASURES, PART 2

"When I first started with Gold Star I had a purchase transaction that seemed to be a slam dunk. The Realtor and client were very happy with us. I had the appraisal scheduled for later in the week but was in the neighborhood so I drove by the property. It had been vacant for a while so the grass and garden were a mess; the house was also filthy. I wanted to make sure everything went off without a hitch so the following day I went to the property with my lawn mower and a lot of cleaning supplies. I thought I was only going to be there for a few hours but I ended up spending the entire day cutting the grass, weeding, and cleaning the inside of the property so when the appraiser took photos, the place looked good. In the end the loan closed on time and there were no issues with the appraisal. The client was very grateful and referred me to his family members down the line."

—Gold Star originator

"A well-known financial services advisor who has many older clients told me he receives a lot of phone calls from his clients' children who live out of state. They are worried about their aging parent and quite often are lost when it comes to selecting an assisted living facility in Michigan. This advisor personally takes his clients and their children to different community living centers in the area, so they could find the right one. He gladly goes an extra mile for his clients without any compensation, stressing that you simply cannot put a dollar value on 'giving back' to your clients. After meeting him and experiencing the level of his service, many of his clients' children choose to keep their account with him even after their parents pass away."

—A Financial Services Consultant

Apparently the client did not realize the importance of the pending deadline and kept postponing his annual withdrawal. When he took a vacation in mid-December, the client neglected to inform his financial advisor who left several phone messages to discuss the situation. However, the concerned financial services representative learned that his client was returning home sometime on December 28, a few days prior to the deadline. He drove to the client's house and waited several hours on the front porch. The client finally arrived, the necessary paperwork was signed and the capital gains issue was successfully resolved.

Dealing with Special Challenges.

A clothing store salesman was faced with an unusual situation when a man came to his store wanting a custom made suit. The customer indicated he had not been very happy with clothing that he had previously purchased elsewhere. He questioned whether this salesman could provide a properly tailored suit. At first glance, it seemed to be an easy fit--except that the customer had a prosthetic right arm. Every tailor had attempted to make a suit that conformed to the man's artificial arm, which resulted in an overall uneven appearance. The salesman suggested he accompany the customer to the manufacturer that made the prosthesis so they could make an arm to fit the suit, instead of trying to make the suit to fit the arm. The company subsequently developed the prosthetic arm to the salesman's specifications, enabling him to make the suit. He had a satisfied customer who also became a good friend. *That was exceptional service.*

I became acquainted with this same salesman, who knows the type of clothing I like and calls me on a regular basis to suggest a new shirt, coat or tie. Then he drives an hour to my home to deliver these items for my approval. In addition, he has arranged speedy tailoring or dry cleaning jobs in order to accommodate my travel schedule. In one instance, he met me at the office early one morning, after I had just arrived from a long business trip. He took my suits, had them cleaned and returned that afternoon so that I could take them on another trip. Most clothing stores would not make such an effort.

Turning lemons (angry calls) into lemonade (sales).

No salesperson enjoys dealing with complaints, but this is actually another opportunity to strengthen ties with customers. I saw this first-hand when I mistakenly received a complaint letter from the Better Business Bureau regarding a past customer who was upset with the lender servicing his loan. The homeowner was extremely frustrated because the lender hadn't paid his property taxes as per the agreement. While I could have simply contacted the BBB and returned the letter, I saw a chance to correct the situation, strengthen our association with a customer and possibly obtain a new loan. I called the customer and explained that while it really wasn't my obligation to get involved, I wanted to help him. I asked if he would withdraw his complaint regarding the lender if I was able to help solve the problem within 24 hours. He enthusiastically agreed and I next contacted the lender that was certainly interested in quickly resolving the problem. Once I was assured the taxes would be paid and everything was in order for future tax payments, I called the customer again to share the good news. I also explained I had noticed his current loan was at a higher rate and that we could refinance it without any closing costs. He was extremely gratified.

Making it A Win-Win.

Exceptional customer service may take a little longer to initiate, but has major benefits for everyone involved. For instance, I know another salesperson who was trying to make a small retail business grow by starting on a wholesale scale. He purchased a truck and started to haul seafood from the East coast for sale to other small retail stores in his market. His objective was to generate enough capital and supply key contacts in order to obtain much larger accounts. He approached a major grocery chain and told them he would take full responsibility for all of their seafood needs in the state. However, they were selling from their meat department and the meat managers wanted nothing to do with fish. So this industrious salesman developed a simple, but time consuming solution—traveling to every store to set up a seafood section and subsequently providing all of the fish, point-of-purchase material and other support. He helped the grocery chain evolve from selling no seafood to making it an important part of their fresh food department, while establishing his own profitable business.

A Few More Opportunities

There are numerous other, slightly less extreme examples of "going the extra mile." For example, one of our loan originators was waiting at a title company when his customer called to postpone the closing, because she was stranded on a roadway with a flat tire. The easy thing to do would have been to cancel and reschedule the appointment. However, the originator drove to the customer's location, took her to the closing, and afterwards returned to her car to change the flat tire.

In another instance, one of our salespeople was handling a purchase loan for a couple that was expecting a baby within the next week. He took care of their loan in the normal fashion and they chose a Thursday afternoon to close at their house. Of course, with the pending arrival of their new child, time was critical. Wednesday night the client went into labor and delivered a baby girl. The new father explained the situation and then asked about their options. Our loan originator mentioned that he and a notary public could go to the hospital during visiting hours and have the docs signed or he could extend the loan at no additional cost to the borrower and we could reschedule. The new father said "Come on by, we aren't going anywhere." So that afternoon the Gold Star loan officer and the notary went to the hospital to get the documents signed and deliver the keys to the family's new house. While they were signing the docs, the originator was allowed to hold the baby girl and was amazed that he was able to be present for such a special experience of his client, creating a bond with this family that is still just as strong. He has since handled several additional loans for this family.

When one of our clients wanted to close on his new house but faced a delay because the seller lived in Nice, France where he couldn't find a notary, we made a quick decision. We arranged to fly the seller to Michigan at our expense, so he could sign the necessary documents. It was an expensive one-day trip, but worthwhile considering the strong relationship we had with our customer.

A friend of mine, Tony Franchi, is the highly regarded national sales manager of a major food distributor. Earlier in his career he was a route salesman and one of his accounts was a small sandwich shop, whose owner insisted on only paying him in cash for the regular deliveries. The store proprietor had developed a trust with his favorite salesman. Of course, when Tony was promoted to manager, responsible for overseeing sales activity in 15 states, he was no longer responsible for handling individual accounts. Yet the sandwich shop owner wanted to continue dealing with him alone. Tony agreed to make a weekly trip—his only remaining sales call— to receive the owner's payment. He did so because he was truly interested in satisfying this loyal customer,

A few of our celebrity clients have even asked us to watch their homes while they are traveling. In one instance, I stopped by a prominent hockey player's house only to find that a pipe had burst and caused flooding in the lower floor. I was able to call a plumber and help avoid further damage.

Establishing Your Own Extra-ordinary Service

Obviously there is no single way to provide exceptional customer service. The key is to make sure you are going beyond the basics to satisfy your customers. Once you have met their essential needs—providing the desired product, reasonable price and best available delivery—look for ways to take it to the next level; for example, by making a house call or providing a "welcome new customer" gift. This may require a little research. Check to see what your competitors are doing: weekend availability, faster turnaround, concierge programs and product guarantees. Ask some of your customers what impresses them most about their salesperson's customer service. You may want to prepare a customer satisfaction survey and e-mail to several past customers.

Some salespeople are limited by their budgets or other restrictions. However, exceptional service doesn't have to be expensive. For example, it might be as simple as devoting extra attention to assure the customer's specific product preferences are available, making a personal delivery or sending a handwritten thank-you card. I generally believe that salespeople should do whatever is necessary to ensure optimum service. If your company doesn't have its own "wow them with service" policy, develop your own now.

Salespeople are (or should be) in control of the transaction, whether it is the sale of an insurance policy, automobile, home loan or computer system. By going beyond the norm, rather than merely following the typical routine, you will make an even more lasting impression that helps to ensure a "lifelong customer."

Chapter Seven
Raising the Bar, to Superstar

"Winning isn't getting ahead of others. It's getting ahead of yourself."
~Roger Staubach.

T HERE ARE NO "BORN" superstars. Rather, it takes a "village" of mentors, sales managers, assistants and other supporting players to help an already successful salesperson mature into a top producer. Sales pros must also possess an abundance of dedication, knowledge, skill and stamina, traits that are typically developed and refined over a period of time.

Many people initially do not have the ability or drive to become a superstar. Maybe they do not know what it takes. Perhaps they lack the desire or confidence, or don't plan far enough ahead. Whatever the reason, they likely will not reach the stratosphere of sales. I certainly didn't think about being a top producer; my primary focus was on having a relatively successful first year. I was too busy to give it much thought. Of course, after achieving a stellar rookie year, I certainly wanted the success to continue.

Evolution of a Superstar

Sales professionals are typically accorded superstar status based on total sales or units. For example, based on industry figures, loan originators closing at least $35 million and 225 loans of personal volume per year could be considered superstars. To be included in the Million Dollar Round Table, insurance salespeople and financial advisors must earn a minimum of $87,900 in first-year commission. (To be eligible for two higher tiers, their annual commission of the first-year income must be three to six times higher than the base requirement.) All salespeople have quotas to reach, including those to be included in the upper echelon of their profession. Obviously, it is difficult to compare successes across professions. A car salesperson has to sell a lot more units to match the dollar volume of a loan originator or yacht broker.

There have always been top producing salespeople, those who set industry records for selling mortgages, cars, paper insurance policies, stocks and a myriad of other products and services. Some can trace their achievement to a combination of knowledge, availability, hard work, market conditions, company visibility, a lack of competition and even a little luck. However, most overachievers have mastered several critical areas that set them apart from the rest. For example: **Joseph Crane**, an early salesman for National Cash Register, based his success on learning everything possible about his prospects' needs and then finding the most effective ways to satisfy them. He knew that by having a better understanding of his customer's current situation and future plans, he would be better able to offer the right product. In today's sales environment, that sounds like such a simple concept. At the time, it was revolutionary sales thinking.

Joe Girard got into the 1973 *Guinness Book of World Records* by selling 1,425 cars. He is widely regarded by many of his peers to be the "world's greatest salesman." He got his start as a nine-year old selling shoe shines and newspapers. Girard later recounted that a turning point in his development as the world's premier car salesman was when he hired an assistant, enabling him to delegate other tasks while keeping his focus on selling. He eventually established several enduring sales techniques, like relationship marketing, and he introduced the well-known Law of 250. The latter emphasizes that we all know at least 250 people, and are thus able to influence each of them, who can then reach another 250 people, and so on, all of whom could be potential sales and referral sources. Of course the other side of the coin is that if you alienate one or more of the 250, your mistake can represent a lot of lost sales!

In order to become top producers in their fields, all salespeople should follow the lessons of Joseph Crane, Joe Girard and others.

Superstar Requirements

It is generally well known that 20 percent of the practicing salespeople generate 80 percent of the total sales. What does it take to become and remain a superstar? This is a question I often pose to novice salespeople who ask for advice. Their typical responses are: "Knowing your product," "serving your customers," "returning customer calls promptly," "not putting your paycheck in front of the customer's needs" and "being honest."

I generally respond that "Those are the basic requirements for all salespeople; what you have to do just to be moderately successful. What about the criteria that enables salespeople to become the best in their profession?" I have found that it is a difficult question for many to answer; even some highly successful salespeople aren't initially able to identify what helped them get to the top. According to an informal survey of top performers, following are the key characteristics that can help salespeople reach impressive production milestones.

Strengthen Your Commitment

Are top producers more committed than average salespeople? Yes. It is not easy to become and remain a superstar. You have to work longer hours, especially in your first few years. You must set and meet demanding goals, thrive during difficult market conditions and always remain confident in your abilities.

Some salespeople are willing to raise the level of their commitment to become a top producer, while others are not ready to make the additional sacrifices and will likely never be among the truly elite. I waited several years and overcame two failures before achieving my first major sales success. I was ready to do whatever was necessary, such as working extremely long hours, to be certain I would continue performing at an optimum level.

Plan for the Long-term

Successful salespeople have a vision that extends beyond the next six months or a year. In addition to achieving short-term goals, you have to look forward five or 10 years. A good place to start in reexamining your goal strategy is to answer four essential questions. Write them on a piece of paper: "Who am I?" "What do I want to be?" "What will it take to get there?" and "Am I willing to do it?" Obviously, you need to have no reservations when you answer "yes" to the final question. Otherwise, it will be difficult to achieve superstar status.

If you determine your ultimate goal is "financial freedom" by a certain age, what will it take to get there? How many completed sales will you need per month and year to reach that goal? What is your closing ratio? If you are able to close 30 percent of the leads you get, how many prospects must you see every month, week and day to reach your goals? This also means anticipating trends and challenges that could impact your development as a top producer. What happens if there is a sudden decrease in demand for your product? How will that impact your initial projections?

After my first high volume year in 2000, I realized I would have to take certain steps to hit higher production numbers in the future. I also learned we can only savor our past success for a brief period before moving forward. I began spending more time with long range planning, anticipating what I would need to do over the next two to five years. I carefully analyzed my operational and marketing strategies to determine what was most effective and how I could improve. I researched demographics and other marketing trends to give me additional insights to help anticipate future customer profiles. I expanded my focus from six-month and one-year planning to a five and 10-year focus.

Get Help Now

You cannot get to the top by yourself. It is nearly impossible to do so without an assistant. Most sales superstars have one or more assistants and form teams so that they can concentrate on business-building activities and delegate other responsibilities. Salespeople often complain that they can't afford to have an assistant. Actually they can't afford not to. The production levels will vary, but once you reach a certain point and are unable to grow further, you need to hire one. It is simple math: if your hourly rate is $50 an hour, you shouldn't be handling the myriad of responsibilities that a $12 an hour assistant can coordinate.

A FAST-PACED OFFICE

I first worked with Dan when I joined Golden Rule and was relatively new to processing; he was an underwriter at InterFirst. Approvals were coming back from InterFirst at lightning speed. We received a complimentary letter from Dan that thanked Golden Rule and the processor for sending such complete and well-documented files.

I met Dan for the first time when he opened the Golden Rule office in Ann Arbor. I saw that he was a young kid young enough to be my son. At the time, I was based in Tampa, assigned to process his loans. Working with Dan was the most demanding, frustrating, profitable and fast-paced time ever. But the loans always closed.

Dan was quick to acknowledge a job well done. He would send me flowers and arrange special lunches after an especially busy week or month. Much later, when my nephew was killed in an accident, Dan called to offer his sympathies. When I told him that my daughter and I might have to travel to California for the service, he told me to use his credit card for the plane fare. I didn't need to use the credit card but was touched by his generosity."

~Donna Rogers, Loan Assistant/ Processor

I hired my first assistant after about a year as a loan originator and should have done so earlier. Before he joined me, I had been helping with many of the office chores that needed to get done but were not directly tied to our production. I was answering all of the phones, ordering supplies and handling a variety of other tasks that also weren't contributing to my sales goals. Once I shifted some of that responsibility to an assistant, my volume rose dramatically. My first and subsequent assistants had an especially difficult job; as the sales activity increased, so did their workload. My second assistant was Angie Fant, who was able to endure the challenging days with patience and a wonderful attitude. In one month alone, she helped me close 181 loans. Angie has been with Gold Star in different capacities for nearly a decade.

Some salespeople are content with one assistant, while others create a team of several assistants and support staff. Others have a difficult time working with an assistant because it interferes with their normal routine. It can be inconvenient during the first few months of training an assistant, when you have to spend extra time to answer their questions and review their work. Before long, though, it should become a smooth running system.

SUPERSTAR VIEWS

"I believe that through experience, top producers generally develop a higher learning skill set than others. They have a better grasp of what to ask customers…"

"Having a team and being able to delegate to them is key. To be able to break through to the next level, you need to surround yourself with good people."

"You have to have an ironclad goal and a plan to achieve it. That requires drive and a work ethic that means you'll do whatever is necessary to achieve your goal."

"I am usually the first in the office and the last to leave."

—(Paraphrased from various top producers)

Other salespeople are afraid to delegate. Their idea is that "No one does it (paperwork, applications and follow-up) as well as I can. I am afraid I'll lose touch with this part of my business." This micromanagement is a shortsighted attitude, and if carried to the extreme means that the salesperson will never be able take a vacation for fear their customers won't be properly serviced. Customers understand and appreciate that top producers need support and that you have to delegate some responsibilities.

If you are still unsure of the merits of hiring an assistant, talk to top producers at your company and elsewhere in your market. Ask those who have an assistant how it has helped increase their production.

Invest in Yourself

Salespeople should view themselves as a business or a mini-corporation, rather than a loan originator, real estate agent or insurance salesman. Do whatever it takes to grow the business. Just as you're willing to hire an assistant to help get you to the next level, it's also important to invest in the business in other ways. For example, salespeople shouldn't necessarily expect their companies to provide laptops, marketing materials and other "necessities." When we first opened the Golden Rule office, I used $3,000 of my own money to cover various overhead expenses, and there have been a number of other instances when I invested my own income for marketing campaigns and other costs. Some management consultants have said that three percent of your annual income is a reasonable amount to invest. Based on my own experience and conversations with other salespeople, I think it should be higher – as much as 20 percent. Of course, you can gradually increase your investment and ultimately, the amount will be what you are comfortable spending. Do your own cost/benefit analysis to ascertain how much you are able to invest to help generate a specific production level.

Work for a Supportive Company

While you must be willing to contribute to your own success, working for a highly supportive company can make a substantial difference. For example, you want to be associated with a firm that has a superior reputation, offers a competitive commission program and provides a comprehensive infrastructure that will enable you to reach desired production levels. Some companies provide marketing assistance. It is also valuable to have a positive environment whereby management recognizes significant achievements. I attribute much of my early success as an originator to Golden Rule's extensive back office services and overall support. Gold Star also provides the foundation enabling our salespeople to grow their business. We provide the training, technology and other appropriate services to help them succeed.

Certainly determining whether or not a company is "supportive" can be a subjective process. But most salespeople know when their company truly has their best interests in mind. If you feel you can't reach the next level of success at your present company, make a change as soon as possible. However, struggling salespeople should avoid completely blaming the company for their lower production. When originators tell me they know that by joining Gold Star they could substantially expand their production, I usually advise them to first increase their sales at the current company.

Think and Reach "Outside the Box"

Top producers constantly seek unique ways to run their business. It may involve implementing new operational or marketing techniques to set them apart from the competition. Offering discounted pricing, developing a professional athlete niche and introducing a special $1 million giveaway promotion were a few of the different approaches we took to generate recognition of Gold Star. When Gold Star held a company-wide managers' meeting, we decided to host a giant tailgate party at a University of Michigan football game. This was more than a welcome gathering for our employees; we wanted to reach a larger audience—many of the 115,000 spectators who were at the newly remodeled stadium that day. We had a giant Gold Star banner and posters made, showcasing our 800-201-LOAN number and our reputation as one of the area's best places to work. We knew that a huge audience of potential customers and employees would see the display. It was well worth our time and investment, as we substantially increased our visibility and had a great time doing so.

Thinking outside the box doesn't necessarily require an excessive budget. When I started as a salesman, I developed an emerging market (immigrant) niche that no one else was exploring at the time. Find your own niche. Research the demographics of your area. Look at the trends of where the population has been and how experts believe it will evolve. If you see that the 65+ population is on the rise, offer programs appealing to that group.

I also placed an emphasis on providing Realtors with referrals before ever asking them for leads, another seemingly basic strategy that my competitors had not adopted. You can start your own celebrity niche on a local scale, by doing business with radio and television station personalities and other well-known people. The point is, you just need to take a more creative approach to your usual routine. Evaluate what you have done in the past and what the competition is doing, then make sure you continually test a few new strategies.

Raise the Bar

Continue to set higher production goals and be relentless in your pursuit of them. While it is important to avoid setting unrealistically high goals and then missing them, you also don't want to sell yourself short with easily achievable goals. Too many salespeople get complacent after reaching a certain production level and are not willing to extend themselves to meet or exceed their goals in future years.

During our first year in business, I remember asking Brink Cawley, "Do you think we can continue producing at this level?" Of course, my enthusiasm was tempered with the realization that rate fluctuations can quickly change the sounds of the office from ringing phones to near silence. Even though I knew I had not come close to realizing my full potential, I was not sure how to forecast for the following year. I did outline what I thought it would take to reach my new target, including the number of new prospects to see and the amount of loans to close. I saw that by spring-boarding from one smaller goal to the next and growing my production incrementally, I would ultimately reach my desired targets. From that point on, I set aggressive *and* realistic sales goals.

Become Even Smarter

Salespeople often stop learning once they reach a certain level. It may be unintentional, but they begin to neglect some of the "study habits" that initially helped them succeed. As one top producer said, "Once you think you know everything about the business, your production will suffer." This is especially true in today's rapidly changing business environment. You have to continue your education so that you become known as the wisest expert in the market. You should possess a thorough understanding of the industry's regulations, market demographics and economic trends. Understand the competition's products and programs better than anyone else. Be able to answer every possible objection customers can raise. During the last few years, I've interviewed a number of unemployed loan originators, many of whom have not continued their education. They and many other salespeople have not kept up with their profession and they aren't the ideal job candidates in today's competitive marketplace.

Customers have become more demanding of salespeople. They expect that you will have answers to *all* of their questions. They are especially impressed when your wisdom helps them understand the "bigger picture," how your counsel will assist them in planning for the future. My own "turning point" as a salesman occurred when I finally acquired a comprehensive knowledge of loan programs, industry guidelines, underwriting criteria and closing techniques that would enable me to effectively serve customers. In order to stay abreast of the many changes to lending and sales, I have since become a voracious reader of sales and management books, in addition to a variety of business magazines.

Of course, it's important that you make sure customers know that you are an expert in your field. There is a humorous story (original source unknown) that illustrates this point.

A frustrated homeowner tried to fix a clogged drain but made an even bigger mess. He called a plumber who took a quick look under the sink and then tapped a pipe with his hammer. Of course, the drain cleared and the homeowner was excited that it was such a simple job. However, he was a bit surprised when the plumber said his fee was $80.50. He complained that the plumber's charge seemed excessive for such a quick fix and asked for an itemized bill. The plumber gladly obliged and on a piece of paper scribbled "$80.50—with fifty cents for the use of my special hammer and $80 for my expertise; knowing just where and how hard to hit the pipe."

Sometimes customers need to be reminded that they do business with you because you have the knowledge to provide them with solutions.

Brand Yourself

You want customers and prospects to recognize you as the one salesperson in your market they should contact. It is fine to be associated with a well-regarded company, but you need to have your own identity as the salesperson that provides value to his or her customers. More salespeople have chosen to refer to themselves as "advisers" or "consultants" as one branding strategy. When we launched the company, we developed an identity as a customer service-oriented lender that provided "affordable mortgages at discounted rates," a branding that we have continued. My own branding evolved as customers and prospects began to recognize me as the nation's top ranked loan originator.

Be sure to avoid branding yourself too narrowly. For instance, developing a reputation as "The First-time Homeowner's Realtor," will substantially reduce your customer base, unless you prefer to only work with new homeowners. Many loan originators who nurtured a "subprime specialist" brand were unable to distance themselves from that unpopular title once the lending industry's crisis unfolded.

Concentrate on Profitable Strategies

Most new salespeople start by focusing on a variety of niche audiences that might have an interest in their product/service. In addition, there is a tendency to engage in diverse marketing activities, including advertising, seminars, direct mail programs and special events.

However, it's crucial to concentrate on programs and niches that are the most profitable. Do your research to determine which potential markets haven't been overexposed, those that the competition hasn't yet developed. Make a detailed analysis of your most profitable activities during the last two years. What has given you the best return on your investment? And bear in mind that this is an ongoing process – what works today may not be as cost-effective tomorrow.

Adapt to Technology

Top producers have a better grasp of the latest technological developments, including Internet marketing and social media techniques. Unlike their techno-phobic counterparts, they are "grad students" of sales-related technology, and look for ways to incorporate it in their operations. Technology is one of the topics we discuss with prospective originators, and I emphasize that we are seeking people who are willing to take advantage of the various Internet and related opportunities.

However, there is a flip side to embracing technology advancements; we can't ignore the human element. In 2001-02, many experts argued that the Internet would soon make loan originators obsolete, that borrowers would find online research and purchases so easy they would no longer see the need to have direct contact with salespeople. Of course, this was a huge miscalculation. Consumers will buy books, CDs, shoes, and a wide variety of other items through online sources. However, when it comes to the major life purchases, such as a home mortgage, automobile, financial planning and life insurance, most people prefer to have an expert with whom they can discuss the details and develop a personal relationship. There is a comfort level provided by personal interaction that a computer screen just cannot match. If a customer is in danger of losing their home or needs some reassuring words about their future needs, knowing that they can talk to me or another salesman makes a big difference.

I recently had an opportunity to counsel one of our loan officer trainees, who had become quite fond of Internet sales. I explained that the way to long-term sales success is creating a bond with customers, making them feel like they are the most important people in your life. "Web-based applications can't explain the process to the customer or discuss their personal situation the way a salesperson can," I stressed. "If you become a Web-only salesman, three months from your closings, nearly 90 percent of your customers won't remember your name. And if they do, they would remember you as my assistant but never as an expert in the finance field."

Build a Never-ending Referral Pipeline

Successful salespeople depend on referrals, rather than always chasing new leads. Obviously, it is good to develop new sources of business generated from advertising or lead lists, but referrals are usually a superstar's main focus. Adhere to this simple concept and your satisfied customers will tell family members, work associates, friends and others to do business with you. That loyal base will continue to expand, and eventually you will be fortunate enough to assist the children of your original customers.

In order to ensure that referrals multiply, you must first ask for them at various stages throughout and after the sales process. Strategic business partners and customers often need to be reminded that you appreciate them referring their friends, neighbors and work associates. Then you must stay in contact with customers on a regular basis so they will continue to refer you to others. I'm surprised that salespeople in various professions ignore this fact: if you don't pay attention to your customers, someone else will. However, I learned early on that as long as I provided customers with an affordable rate and personalized service, an expensive mailing campaign was not necessary. Staying in touch several times a year, through a brief letter or phone call, is usually sufficient.

Find a Mentor

Novice salespeople should seek a mentor who can share proven strategies and help avoid the inevitable obstacles. The mentor is typically an experienced salesperson at your company who is willing for you to "shadow" them, but it could also be a salesperson/manager somewhere else.

I have benefited from a mentor's support at various stages of my career. People such as the Owens' took extra time to offer me proven ideas that had helped them gain their measure of success. Although I opened a branch of one mortgage company and later launched a new firm, I continue to seek the guidance of mentors, people who have more business experience than I do. I talk to these advisers on a regular basis about legal issues, management directions and other critical topics. In addition, I make certain that I provide a mentor's support to others – not only Gold Star salespeople, but originators from around the country who call for advice.

Motivate Yourself

Self-motivation is one of the major factors in maintaining super-stardom; you have to have the drive to stay a top performer. During the last few years, I've seen a number of salespeople who seem to have lost their inspiration. They were once top producers, but have since run out of steam. Many are the "older" salespeople who have suffered through the economic downturn and are hanging on for a while longer until they can retire or move on to another profession. They're worn out from the daily obstacles, and their production has noticeably declined.

BECOMING A TOP PRODUCER

"Successful salespeople are competitive. We want to win at everything."

"The main thing is being different from others. It's good to step outside the box and give customers another reason to use you."

"You always have to ask where your business is going to be in the next three to six months."

"You can't afford to get sidetracked with non-essential activities."

"You have to be available 24 hours a day, seven days a week to get to the next level."

—From top producing salespeople.

Obviously, companies want to make sure that their salespeople stay motivated. They provide financial incentives, and their sales managers offer direction and encouragement. I also believe that attending conferences and motivational seminars can be beneficial, providing salespeople with a needed "boost," as long as they actually implement some of the advice. Too often they attend these events and get excited about the speaker's suggestions for greater success, then forget to follow the directions once they return to the office. Salespeople must create their own formulae to stay motivated.

For many, earning an income to support their family's diverse needs is sufficient motivation. My personal drive is fueled by a passion for sales and a long-standing desire to achieve.

Maintain a Strong Work Ethic

Newer salespeople are typically willing to work extra hours to reach their goals, reasoning that they can slow down once they reach the upper level. I have talked with numerous salespeople who exclaim "Once I hit $xx million in production, I am going to cut back and not work as much." However, the most successful have learned that in today's competitive environment, it is more difficult to substantially reduce their workday if they want to retain their market share. There is nothing wrong with taking long vacations and leaving early to play golf, but that is not necessarily the formula for superstar status.

In my first few years as an originator, I worked 80-100 hour weeks and was available on the weekends. I no longer work the same schedule, but I haven't slowed my overall approach. I still work with the same intensity while in the office. I haven't taken a sick day in more than 12 years. I believe that as you gain experience as a salesman, you find ways to "get more out of each day," by working smarter.

Don't Get Burned

Studies confirm that a high percentage of many companies' salespeople and other employees suffer from burnout. They feel stressed, their production drops and in many cases they leave to find a different company or a new profession. I've seen many top producers at other companies hit a "brick wall" brought on by various factors. The salesman becomes frustrated at his declining volume, the firm's poor customer service program, and many other real and perceived reasons.

The key is to catch the signs of burnout early and take corrective actions. First, make the necessary work-related adjustments; upgrade operating systems, develop better relationships with strategic partners, increase customer-follow-up and enhance your marketing strategies. Then if necessary, create the appropriate balance between your work and personal lives; watch your kid's soccer/football games, take a vacation and/or get involved in community activities. Gold Star is demanding of our originators and support staff, but we also make sure that there is a family-oriented environment to help eliminate burnout. We watch for signs of this common problem and do whatever we can to help originators and staff avoid it.

It is difficult to become a top producing salesperson, and harder still to remain at that level year after year. Aspiring superstars should learn the lessons of top salespeople, how they evolved from moderate success to become a mega-producer. Following their path won't guarantee super-stardom; however you will have a much greater chance of realizing your long-term goals.

Chapter Eight

Lunch is for Losers

"If you want to make good use of your time, you've got to know what's most important and then give it all you've got."

~Lee Iacocca

"I don't know how I can get it all done," and, "There just aren't enough hours in the day!" must be two of the most often repeated phrases by new and veteran salespeople.

While working an 18-hour day is one way to ensure you can tackle a never-ending "to do" list, most people are either unwilling or unable to follow that schedule, so they look for a proven system to help make each day more productive.

There are numerous business management gurus who promote seemingly fail-safe guidelines for work success, but these techniques do not always apply to everyone. For example, many experts insist that time blocking is the answer to enhancing your organizational effectiveness. Time blockers designate a specific period of time each day to accomplish certain tasks. They reason that you will achieve maximum efficiency by scheduling an hour in the morning for phone calls, followed by 1 ½ hours for staff meetings, and two hours for customer contact, and one hour for returning e-mails, and so on. The problem is that this is often too regimented and inflexible for most high volume producers. If you are in the phone call hour and a valuable customer visits unexpectedly, do you stay with phone calls or meet with the customer? During your staff meetings do you ignore calls and let them accumulate until you have a long list of callbacks? Time blocking is effective for people with a fairly set work schedule that lacks many unexpected challenges, but is not necessarily ideal for those who are faced with a daily barrage of interruptions. I tried time blocking in my early days as a loan originator, and found that I often became more concerned about keeping a predetermined schedule than I was about accomplishing my daily tasks.

My time management system is simpler than most. Every evening I make a handwritten list of what I want to accomplish the following day, often waking up late at night to add a few new items. Of course, I realize that my list will most likely expand significantly with a series of "follow-up ASAP" notations and "don't forget to" reminders. I do use a BlackBerry to keep track of key action items, but I still rely on the written list. I review the daily assignments on my 45-minute ride to work, while also talking to clients, assistants and business partners. On one winter morning I was driving to a meeting with one of our sales managers. During the ride I was going through my usual routine of calls, lists and e-mails. I just finished a call to a customer when my passenger said: "I just saw you do more in an hour than most people get done in a week." A little hyperbole perhaps, but it does underscore my emphasis on packing the most into each day. The morning commute to work enables me to get some of my "to do" list done and helps put me in the best working mindset. I think most salespeople could benefit from a self-motivational pep talk so that they look forward to the day, rather than wasting energy dreading the tasks they face.

Once at the office, I close the door on my personal issues—a needed plumbing repair, weekend plans, and other potential distractions—to concentrate on my mission of closing more transactions and helping manage the company. As soon as I sit down, I begin taking calls from a wide variety of people anxious clients, prospects, lenders, Realtors, and Gold Star salespeople and support staff. Throughout the day I juggle a myriad of management tasks along with my own sales activity. While I now spend only about 40 percent of my day on personal sales, this remains the part about which I am most passionate. Making sales enables me to stay connected to the lifeblood of the company. After all, I realized a major goal when I finally became a top-producing originator, and I have always been fascinated by the wide variety of sales situations, from the mundane to the highly complex. I especially enjoy talking with prospects who challenge me with a series of objections or questions before we reach an agreement. I never get tired of hearing something similar to "You've answered all of my questions and I'm ready to do business." I am convinced that if salespeople can maintain this same enthusiasm, the excitement about being challenged by prospective customers, they will never grow tired of their job.

I strongly believe that sales managers must continue to sell at some level; otherwise it is difficult to relate to their salespeople and there is a tendency to become insulated from customers. All of our top managers originate loans on a regular basis, which helps them better understand the everyday challenges of today's customer and also creates a stronger bond among their salespeople. Producing managers are a unique breed of people who have a special skill set and temperament. They are able to juggle the demands of their own sales activity while being responsible for overseeing the actions of a group of other salespeople and staff or an entire office. They are typically top producers who their company wants to lead other salespeople to greater success.

Adding Variety

I usually add a few special responsibilities to my daily routine. For example, I help sort and deliver mail to headquarters staff several times a week. We do have administrative staff members who are probably more effective at distributing the mail, but this extra duty gives me a chance to "make the rounds" and talk to those I might not otherwise see that day, while taking a quick break from the phones. In addition, I enjoy leading prospective employees and customers on occasional tours, so that they can see the energy throughout the office.

After I make the elevator speech about Gold Star's history and mission, I introduce our guests to key people and suggest applicants meet with one or more of our loan originators "behind closed doors." This is the part they seem to especially enjoy because it offers a chance to get an uncensored opinion of Gold Star, without my presence. They seem to appreciate that we are not trying to give them a sanitized view of our company. Several new hires have later told me their decision to join us was at least partially influenced by that chance to have informal discussions with managers and other personnel.

CONTROLLED CHAOS

"Throughout a 'typical' day, Dan will be reading e-mails, checking his BlackBerry, talking to customers on one of three constantly ringing phones and meeting with various people—all at the same time. He talks and moves fast; it's a very quick pace from the beginning of each day to the end. To an outside observer, this might seem chaotic, but it really isn't. Dan expects things to be done quickly. I consider myself to be highly organized, and good at multitasking. I always have a variety of projects under way at the same time. It's often like a chess game, anticipating what needs to be done next.

"Despite his busy schedule, Dan is very approachable; he always has time to spend with employees who stop by with a question or want to share some information."

—Kim Richter, Dan's Assistant

I also assume the role of Gold Star cheerleader whenever possible, which often involves an incentive or motivational campaign. These actions are usually planned in advance, though at other times they are more spontaneous. During one of my daily walks throughout the office, I stopped by our post-closing department to thank them for their hard work and ask for a little extra effort. We already had a substantial bonus in place, but I wanted to add something special. "If you do an additional $5 million by Friday, I will give you each a gift certificate to IHOP (International House of Pancakes)," I announced, knowing that they often joked that this was their favorite restaurant. Later that day, I walked by their office and saw an IHOP menu posted on the door and on their computer screens, so I knew then that they had embraced my challenge. Believing they were capable of even greater results and wanting to motivate them further, I decided to increase the incentive. "If you hit $10 million beyond the target, I will actually serve you breakfast," I explained. I was sure this would be an impossible target and Friday morning they were still $2 million short of the revised goal, so I had no worry about becoming a temporary IHOP waiter.

I obviously underestimated my team. Approaching their office at 5 p.m., I heard them cheering – they had reached the seemingly unattainable goal. I contacted the IHOP manager to ask for permission to serve my staff breakfast there. He was amused at my request but agreed to allow me to wear an IHOP apron and fulfill my promise. This somewhat unusual incentive accomplished financial and motivational objectives. Of course, it helped boost the company's total revenue, but more important, it fostered additional camaraderie, the team spirit for which all companies strive.

THE WHIRLY CART COMPETITION

(We are serious about our work, although we do find time to have fun.)

TO: Whirly Cart Competitors

RE: Upcoming Contest

After 72 hours of intense debate, we have the results of the Whirly draft, which I know you are looking forward to.

We have selected five teams of enthusiastic Whirly Cart competitors, some with more experience than others (I was surprised to learn that a few of you have been practicing lately).

There will be six games played. The final game will be determined by the two teams with the highest amount of points…or whoever is left and able to drive the Whirly Cart.

We have yet to determine the prizes for this once-in-a-lifetime (or at least this year) contest, but I can promise you will be overwhelmed.

On another occasion, I joined our managers and salespeople for an unusual whirly cart competition at a local entertainment center. I may not have been the most accomplished cart driver that evening—mainly because I was driving with one hand while talking business on my phone—but I was definitely one of the most enthusiastic and vocal supporters of the Gold Star team.

The Training Table

I devote a portion of each day to our training program for new salespeople, providing them with support that was lacking in my earliest sales days. I tell the selected trainees that for their first six months at Gold Star, they will sit at one of the desks in my personal office so that they can learn all facets of our business. They listen and watch how I speak to customers and lenders, hear how I review loan programs and handle problems, and generally begin preparing to develop their own business—all under my close supervision. Of course, it isn't always easy for them as I observe and critique their phone calls and other work. But these novice salespeople know that when they have finished the 12-month training, they will be well prepared for success and assured of earning a nice income.

Several of our sales managers also serve as trainers, but I felt that this is one of the best ways for me to continue sharing some of the crucial lessons I would have welcomed as a fledgling originator. The arrangement may seem like an inconvenience—as my office often becomes a noisy workroom—but there has rarely been a problem. Moreover, it definitely helps them and our bottom line: they assist me in closing more loans, and as a company we retain loyal employees who appreciate our investment in their future. I have personally gained a great deal from this sales training as well. For example, while others consider me to be a demanding (but fair) CEO, I believe I have become more patient as a result of working closely with new salespeople on a daily basis. I have also developed an even greater appreciation for the personal challenges with which people deal, and the importance of recognizing individual achievements.

To make this training table concept work, you have to screen candidates carefully. I typically look for recent college graduates who want to learn, are willing to work hard and committed to devoting long hours for an initial modest income. I make sure they understand what is required, that they will be working with one or more other trainees in "close quarters." Not everyone is receptive to the regimen.

CRASH COURSE

I originally interviewed with Gold Star on a momentous occasion. We were in the conference room with several managers when suddenly everyone was silent. Someone pointed to the TV in the corner and we heard the surprising announcement. Bear Stearns, one of the nation's largest investment banks, was shutting down, soon to be absorbed by JP Morgan Chase.

My first day at Gold Star was two days after my graduation from college. I walked in and my desk was set up in Dan's office aside two other interns. I learned my basic mortgage skills in that office. When I started, Dan would call us around his desk and put a sales call on speakerphone. We would listen in silence as he sold the loan and then he would go over key points after (sometimes while the phone was muted). In between sales call training I was assigned to post-closing condition clearing. This was a great place for me to learn what goes into a file, how the systems work, what it takes to get a mortgage and even how to talk to business partners. I started selling during my third month at Gold Star.

We were given leads to call, as well as inbound sales calls that we would take in the office. Dan would critique the call after (and during) to help instill the basics of selling.

—AJ Franchi, Gold Star

You also have to provide a structured environment to accomplish the "curriculum;" a set list of strategies, skills and other lessons that you wish to impart. For example, the lessons include basic product knowledge, phone skills, customer interaction, and closing techniques. It is a mistake to use these trainees solely as personal assistants—running errands without giving them any foundation to be a successful salesperson.

Customer Calls

I have a well-deserved reputation for carrying on multiple phone conversations simultaneously. Unlike other companies, Gold Star eschews the use of voice mail. My belief is that if the phone has rung three times, it has rung two times too many. People shopping for a product or service typically do not want to wait for a call-back; they will find another salesperson who can offer the same item. If our originators aren't able to take a call at their desk, it goes direct to their cell phone, which they are encouraged to answer right away. I have two desk phones, a BlackBerry and another cell phone, and all are usually ringing throughout the day. When I am speaking with a customer or lender and another phone rings, I will ask the first caller if they want me to call them back or if they can hold for a minute; they usually want to wait. Then I will see if I can briefly help the second caller or ask them to hold or wait for a return call, then return to the initial conversation. Frequently I will have three to five calls under way at the same time; my record is 11 simultaneous conversations.

Of course, I also have assistants to help manage incoming calls, but the point is that I strive to get clients' answers and address their concerns immediately, rather than having a long list of return calls. It is a more efficient use of time and also impresses customers when they think you are handling their issue right away. During the last decade, I have refined my multiple call strategy so that I am able to answer each caller's questions and make recommendations *briefly* and *personally*. I have learned to get to the point quickly, assess the caller's immediate situation, and determine what additional information is required.

Lunch is For Losers

There is another major part of my daily routine, lunch in the office. I almost never go out to lunch – not with a Realtor, lender or Gold Star loan originator. That is because **lunch is for losers,** which might sound extreme but is actually a very solid concept. I first recognized the benefits of in-office lunches shortly after opening the Golden Rule office. Up to that point, I had been so busy working with customers and developing our systems that I didn't have time to leave the office for anything. One day, a sales associate went out to lunch while I continued to talk with customers and prospects. During his brief break I obtained three new clients. When he returned, I kidded him that "While you were away, I took all the calls, a few of which would have been yours. I hope your hamburger was worth the $3,000 (commission)." From then on, he was more hesitant about going out to lunch, and I was convinced that desk lunches were profitable.

Salespeople often believe that they need to take their major clients and referral partners to lunch as a way of cementing relationships. It usually isn't required. Most customers appreciate that you are busy and work through lunch. It shows you are popular, an experienced expert with whom they want to do business. Realtors, builders, attorneys and other strategic partners know that I am always available to take their calls.

Of course, we do not have a company policy that prohibits people from going out to lunch. Rather, I and other managers emphasize how valuable time in the office can be. We lead by example, and other salespeople see that by leaving the office to get a hamburger or salad, they might miss one or two sales calls and lose substantial revenue. Originators understand that many consumers do their research and make purchases during *their* lunch time and will often call another salesman if their first contact isn't available. We have found that our loan originators thrive on the "working lunch" environment, knowing that their dedication will be well rewarded. This is part of the "working smarter" mindset that salespeople seem to understand and appreciate. As a survey from Right Management and LinkedIn has confirmed, fewer than half of workers leave their desk to eat lunch. Other studies have emphasized the importance of getting away from your desk during the workday. However, there are other ways to do this, such as long coffee breaks or a walk around the office building, without being absent during the valuable lunch hour. I understand that many people—including some readers—may still think the **Lunch is for Losers** attitude is too harsh and closely associated with a boiler room operation, so I am willing to soften it somewhat to **Salespeople Who Take the Regular Lunch Hour are Losers – of Additional Income.**

In addition to working through lunch, I rarely leave the office for any other reason. This actually started when I resumed selling after my earlier two failures. I was 24 and looked even younger. I felt that Realtors or builder representatives who were considerably older would relate my youthful appearance with inexperience. I developed my early business from referrals and several productive niches, which didn't require me to make office stops. Now that I'm older and no longer have to worry about appearances, I am able to rely on my pipeline of referrals.

Of course, I understand that salespeople do need to leave their offices. While we encourage customers to visit our offices, obviously this isn't always possible. Our customer service pledge ensures that we will meet with them at their home or office. In addition, many salespeople develop their initial base by being "on the road" to meet with clients. One of our originators is a former professional golfer who decided to switch careers. One of his effective techniques of enhancing relationships with real estate agents is providing them with golf lessons. So if it is a true business building activity, it makes sense to leave the office.

Keeping the Door Open

My regular schedule is interrupted numerous times every day because of the wide open door policy I observe. Many companies claim to have an open door attitude, but in reality it often amounts to little more than managers and executives spending a few minutes each day talking to their employees. From the beginning, Gold Star has had a family atmosphere and I wanted to nurture that environment as much as possible. I encourage all of our employees to call or stop by if they have a question, concern or suggestion. In addition, twice a week I invite one of them for lunch in my office, during which they can ask questions about the company or whatever else is on their mind.

In addition to maintaining rapport with them, the open door policy emphasizes my dislike of scheduling unnecessary meetings. I believe that companies waste too much time in such conferences. It is an easy trap to fall into: someone calls with a question or concern and you respond, "Let's get together at 2 p.m. this afternoon," which ultimately becomes an hour session. I would much rather take the time to meet briefly when the issue is still "hot."

In order to accommodate the unannounced staff visits, I probably take multi-tasking to an extreme. I could be answering one of my 500 daily e-mails and talking on the headset phone when I hear someone ask, "Dan, do you have a minute?" I'll nod and invite them in. I am always interested in their questions, concerns and suggestions, and make a sincere effort to avoid answering e-mails and phone calls during our meeting.

Non-Negotiables

Like other business professionals, I have developed a series of non-negotiables that I must complete every day. There is no compromising, no negotiating to reduce this master action list, even on the busiest days. These daily responsibilities include:

- Finish my basic "to do" checklist
- Exercise every morning (with personal trainer).
- Complete/close at least five loans.
- Return all phone calls.
- Provide appropriate customer/Realtor updates.
- Congratulate other people for their achievements.
- Meet with everyone who has a question, concern or suggestion.
- Enjoy the day—have some fun.

During the last decade, I have become more disciplined in the way I complete my non-negotiables. In my earlier mortgage profession positions, I treated it as the common "to do" list—a lengthy inventory of phone calls, customer contacts, reports and other tasks. I was probably content to complete 75 percent of them, saving the rest for the following day. I gradually realized that non-negotiables also include the more challenging goals, as well as some that are more intangible, such as enjoying the day and acknowledging others' successes. In addition, I became more committed to fulfilling all of them.

All salespeople should have a similar list of non-negotiables that must be completed before the end of their day. It is the best way to hold yourself accountable for the areas you consider most important to the development of your business. Professional coaches stress that this is a key to becoming more successful.

My workday has significantly changed during the last 10 years, with more e-mails, calls, and people to manage, and fewer hours spent directly with customers. Still, as I leave for home each evening, I sincerely look forward to the following day. I reflect on what our entire company and I have accomplished, and on what we have to look forward to. I never want to lose that enthusiasm.

▲

Born in Kiev, Ukraine, to proud parents, Peter Milstein and Diana Khiterer, life was lived in a single-bedroom, 335 sq. ft. apartment in a five-story brick building.

A picture of me as a toddler, one of the few hastily packed items before our departure for the US. We were allowed just one suitcase per person and aged 16, I was ▶ *determined to pack mine to the hilt.*

▲
My parents, brother, Alex, and I on our new start in a new country. Like all immigrant families, ours was well aware of what we had left behind and how much opportunity this country provides to anyone with the will to "be somebody some day."

What better way to discover free enterprise and to learn the ropes of what it means to be customer-focused than at McDonalds? Like actor Eddie Murphy's role in "Coming to America," my first assignment was to clean the bathrooms! Still, as with every job, I knew it was important to do it "to the best of my ability". My parents instilled that mantra in me.

White-collar worker at last! On the path to becoming a successful mortgage banker, I began at TCF Bank and quickly gained valuable experience managing a Comerica branch in a local supermarket and then as an underwriter at InterFirst/ABN Amro Bank. I learned lessons from both successes and failures.

In a 300-square foot office (used as a closet by the previous occupant), in a building not far from Michigan Stadium. After two failures, I started a Michigan branch of Florida's Golden Rule Mortgage. With my first two employees, we were going gangbusters working on the slimmest of margins, but fully dedicated to meeting customers' needs better than anyone else. Later expansion demanded build out of the office and so I originated a loan for the contractor in exchange for work he did. All part of being creative.

In 2001-2002, the Detroit Red Wings signed on Pavel Datsyuk. The young Datsyuk had no credit and needed a place to live. I used my relationships to get him a loan for his first home, for which he was very grateful. That season he helped the Red Wings to a Stanley Cup win. The same season his daughter, Elizabeth (right), and mine, Julie, were born just two weeks apart. Six years later both girls are seen adorning the reclaimed Stanley Cup and "Pasha" has gone on to become not only a good friend but also one of the best hockey players of all time.

In 2009, in the depths of the worst mortgage crisis in living memory, we had to get innovative. I underwrote a promotion with the Detroit Red Wings that cost just $6,000. Over 30,000 people entered their information on our website for a chance to win $1million if the Red Wings scored a goal exactly as many minutes before the end of the first, second, or third periods as our posted interest rate. Additionally, the numerous media outlets nationally that covered this story made sure the hundreds of thousands of people knew who we were.

In 2009, Gold Star Mortgage Financial Group was going from strength to strength. That got us noticed, but I'm especially proud of what the company accomplished in earning the distinction of becoming an Inc. 500 company—one the 500 fastest growing companies in America! A testament to the hard work and efforts of the entire Gold Star "family" and in no small way, a ringing endorsement for the land of opportunity.

It was at the ceremony for the Inc. 500 awards that I met and befriended one of my heroes, Chris Gardner. For those few of you who don't know the name, he's the author and central character in the book "The Pursuit of Happyness," which was made famous by Will Smith's stellar rendition as Chris's character in the movie of the same name. Chris's book and his inspiring words gave me the encouragement to write my own.

10 years and going strong! We recently celebrated our tenth anniversary of the founding of Gold Star Mortgage Financial Group. Also going strong are our first two employees, Brink Cawley and Elena Vaduva. With our strong values and dedication to putting the customer first, we've emerged stronger than ever. It's a testament to our appeal as a place to work that our first two employees are still with us and we were named a Detroit Free Press Top Workplace in 2010.

My brother Alex, a highly successful Realtor, has an amazing work ethic and seems to have a 24/7 schedule. He is masterful at using his extensive network of non-real estate contacts.

My parents and me at Gold Star's annual holiday party, December 2007—16 years after my family arrived in the U.S. I delivered my annual speech to co-workers and business partners, which turned out to be in the middle of the country's worst financial crisis.

Summer vacation of 2009 in Northern Michigan with my daughter, Julie

Chapter Nine
Who is That Mystery Shopper?

"I have been up against tough competition all my life. I wouldn't know how to get along without it."

~Walt Disney

I F YOU DON'T KNOW HOW your competitors answer their phones, you may be in trouble.

It is absolutely essential to understand how the competition operates. You cannot effectively sell your product or service if you don't know how salespeople at other firms are selling. That means knowing how they explain their company's product and program features, respond to consumer questions, deal with objections and much more.

I am convinced that most salespeople don't take advantage of some of the basic intelligence gathering "tools," including mystery shopping, which I first experienced as a McDonald's management trainee. One of our tasks was to visit various outlets and see how the staff handled their drive-thru and walk-in responsibilities. We would evaluate their customer greetings, food quality, delivery time, and other critical areas. In hindsight, I am not sure that we were the most objective judges, but we did our best, and it was a great learning experience. The regional managers also conducted mystery shopping research to see how well everyone performed.

Years later as a new loan originator, I realized that the best way for me to understand my competition was to mystery shop other companies. I would call XXX Mortgage Lending and ask for a loan originator. When he said, "Yes Mr. Jones, how can I help?" I mentioned my interest in a purchase or refinance and asked about their rates, fees, special programs, closing schedules and everything else a customer might want to know. The responses varied greatly, with each call providing valuable insights about the competition. In addition to the basic information gleaned from these conversations, I also listened carefully to how they presented themselves. For example, whether they sounded interested, impatient or condescending, the kind of responses that can quickly influence a caller's decision to do business. All of this data helped me refine my own customer presentation.

It's Basic Training

We have made mystery shopping a staple of Gold Star's overall sales strategy. All new originators are assigned to mystery shop during their first days on the job. They develop a specific scenario and call a number of companies. For example, they introduce themselves as a first-time buyer relocating to that particular city, seeking a $250,000 mortgage, putting 10 percent down and expecting to close the loan in 28 days. Then they listen carefully to the lender's responses, offer a few objections, evaluate each call's strengths and weaknesses, and use the appropriate information to prepare their own "talking points" script.

From our experience, the responding salespeople generally can be described in one of three categories:

- Extremely knowledgeable and helpful. They listen to the mystery shopper's questions, inquire about their current situation and future plans, answer objections, and appear genuinely interested in providing the best possible solution.

- Somewhat knowledgeable, not quite as attentive. These salespeople focus more attention on their latest products and spend less time discussing customer needs. At least they appear interested and answer most of your questions.

- Inept and abrupt. They are not nearly as knowledgeable as their counterparts. They sound rushed, not able or willing to answer customers' questions in detail. These salespeople are often overly aggressive in getting you to commit without having all of the appropriate information. They are the type customers generally prefer to avoid.

Many salespeople probably would be distressed at how they are perceived by their prospects. One of our experienced originators recalled when he mystery shopped a major lender and talked to a loan officer who seemed to reveal his true motivation. "The salesperson who answered was very short with me, so I took it upon myself to dive into the call even more--asking about rates, my house and what I would qualify for," he explained. "The loan officer gave me the greatest picture of the loan program and sent me paperwork while we were on the phone so I could review costs. He mentioned the fees and an interest rate I thought was a little high. I asked, 'Why are you charging me an origination fee?' He responded: 'Well sir, just like you, I have to make money, my base salary doesn't support my spending habits.' I was shocked. I wondered if he actually got clients by making them feel guilty."

Some salespeople use mystery shopping to expand their knowledge of their industry. "During my training period at another company, I made several calls to other lenders and acted like a customer to literally teach myself how to better understand mortgages," one of our originators announced during a sales meeting. "I would call and ask them all sorts of questions like what was an escrow account, when do I need one, is it mandatory and so on. I did this for months because I think my trainer wasn't helping much. So this was actually the best training I could have had."

Mystery shopping is also advantageous when you are introducing a new product or entering a different market. When Gold Star was first considering opening an office in Minnesota, we wanted to be sure our pricing was in line with other lenders. We believed that our "affordable mortgages at discounted rates" concept would be appealing to Minnesota borrowers, yet calls to several area lenders indicated that they might have an even lower price structure. However, after making a few additional calls, we realized that while a few of the state's major lenders were promoting "no points" programs, they were also adding excessive origination fees. Based on this research, we were able to easily adapt our normal approach to be competitive in this new market.

Mystery shopping research can be especially helpful when you are meeting with a prospect who is already working with another company. "We make it a practice to do it (shop) regularly and share the information with our entire region to keep everyone updated on our competition's latest practices, strengths and weaknesses," the vice president of a major Midwest firm told me. "It becomes essential when you are going in to visit a customer who you know uses one of your specific competitors. You have to know what you are up against, and how you can sell against them in order to earn their business. It has always been effective and will remain an essential part of selling."

When one of our originators says they are having a sales-related challenge, I'll usually smile, point to the phone and ask "When did you last mystery shop your competitors?" When they reply that they haven't done so, I quickly stress what they are missing. "If you haven't mystery shopped yet, you're about two years behind, so get started today." As further incentive, I remind them that I still mystery shop several times a week.

Since the early 1940s, the popularity of mystery shopping has increased dramatically. There are a number of companies that provide mystery shopping services and there is even a trade association representing them. The research technique is widely used in retail, car dealerships, hotels, restaurants and other industries.

Lessons Learned

There is a learning curve inherent in the mystery shopping process. For example, one of our new originators had just begun his calls and was talking to a lender who wondered, "If you're a lender, why call us (the lender) to ask these questions?" Of course, our enthusiastic shopper realized that caller I.D. had revealed his name. He quickly finished the call and found the solution—block caller I.D.—then left the office on an errand. Upon his return an hour later, I stopped him and asked loudly, "Any idea why we haven't received any calls, not a single customer or prospect, since you've been out? That's especially alarming considering we ran a newspaper ad this weekend." His puzzled expression confirmed that he didn't have the answer.

MYSTERY SHOPPER TIPS

- *Create a list of typical customer questions that will elicit the most revealing information.*

- *Contact a list of 20-25 of your competitors, including those frequently profiled in local newspaper articles, mentioned by your customers, and with whom you are otherwise familiar.*

- *Allow the other salesperson to do most of the talking, to see how they handle customer calls.*

- *Pose a couple of objections ("I think it's better to wait until interest rates decrease further...," or "I understand that XXX Realty only charges xx% commission...," or "I'm really looking for a more full-service firm, offering insurance and CPA...," etc.) to see how the salesperson deals with the unexpected.*

- *Compile a summary of the responses, evaluate the best and worst.*

- *Use appropriate ideas to create your own script.*

Later that day, the sales manager from our unsuccessfully mystery-shopped competitor called me with an unusual announcement: "For the last hour we've been getting calls from people wanting to talk with you. It's great that we're getting all of these inquiries, but most of them really want you." After some additional checking with our phone system, we found the cause of these misdirected calls. When attempting to block caller I.D. on his prior mystery shopping exercise, our originator inadvertently set the call forwarding code, ensuring that all incoming calls were sent directly to the competitor.

Mystery shoppers also have to be careful about the personal information they provide. Another Gold Star originator was contacting various lenders to obtain their rates and other details. He spent a full day speaking with different representatives from online and local lenders. He finally walked into my office, sat down and said in a concerned voice, " Dan, I have been calling all these companies and having them run scenarios for me and then reviewing the presentations. The last guy said my credit score was almost 100 points less than where it was when I started the day." I looked up and asked, "Have you been giving these companies your social security number?" He nodded sheepishly and responded, "Of course, how else would I get their rates and programs?" He ultimately had 15 different companies run his credit, which severely damaged his record. It took him several weeks to have all the inquiries removed. A good tip for mystery shoppers – Don't give out your SSN.

I learned my own valuable lesson, to use a different name when mystery shopping. During a presentation to our sales team, I called a Connecticut lender to inquire about their programs, rates and overall service. "I'm in Hartford (CT) and just found a property that I'd like to close on as soon as possible," I began. "I want to see if you can help me."

"I'm sure we can," the loan officer said. "Can I get your name?"

"Daniel Milstein," I answered.

There was a brief pause and then, "*The* Dan Milstein?"

"Yes," I replied, happily surprised that he would know my name, but also aware that I would not gather much intelligence from this call. I sensed some irritation as the loan officer advised me that he wouldn't be able to help me after all.

Other Competitive Insights

Mystery shopping is probably the most valuable competitive information technique, but there are several others. In addition to contacting the industry partners with whom you work to gain their insights, you can:

- **Talk to customers**—Ask a few of your long-time customers what they think about your major competitors. Perhaps they have received interesting marketing information or phone calls from one or more of them. They will often have an objective viewpoint.

- **Conduct basic Internet research**—Most salespeople don't do enough Internet sleuthing. A quick check can provide critical details: pricing, product offering, marketing and other useful facts.

- **Call the BBB**—The Better Business Bureau can advise whether or not any complaints have been filed against specific companies.

- **Query the Chamber of Commerce**—Ask the chamber or similar organization to refer five companies in your product/service category and see if you are on the list. Or ask for their views of your two primary competitors.

Know Your Share

Having competitive information can help you better understand how to sell against other salespeople, and in some cases assess your market share. You should know how you measure up against the top salespeople in your area. Some professions, including mortgage lending and insurance, have industry-wide yardsticks that help salespeople gauge their success. For example, several mortgage lending trade publications have ranked loan originators on the basis of their annual production, which confirmed that I was among the top 10 loan originators nationwide over a ten-year period. The Million Dollar Roundtable is one measure of life insurance advisers' standing in their industry. Real estate companies rank their agents based on units sold and total sales. Even where such benchmark information isn't readily available, you can obtain some of the sales data from local business groups, business journals, industry associations and other sources.

Your ranking in the marketplace also should account for how you match the competition in non-production statistics, such as best pricing, response time and customer service. Even though you may want to outshine other salespeople in terms of units sold, it is advantageous to surpass them on these points as well. Survey your customers to get their impressions regarding these areas.

Competitive Alliance

When I started the Golden Rule office, we were definitely the underdog, and were committed to outperforming both small and large firms in our market. Even when there were only two of us, we worked hard to make better deals, be more innovative and work harder than the "big boys." I remembered the phrase "Keep your friends close and your enemies even closer," which had been popular when I was growing up in oppressive Russia, and for a while that was part of our overall business philosophy. I did not want to alienate any other mortgage banker or broker, never knowing whether one day we might have an opportunity to work together in some way. As Golden Rule became better known and we were no longer the same small fish in the big pond, I developed a broader view of competition. For instance, I had an even greater awareness that to succeed at the highest level in this and any other business, you have to be ready to run a marathon rather than a relay race against some very experienced people, many of whom would love to see you fail.

While establishing our own model, I became a student of what other firms were doing. During my career, I have learned a great deal from competitors, some very successful and others that struggled, including those that were forced to shut down during the lending industry crisis. I have gained insights about effective marketing techniques, operational strategies and additional areas by reading industry publications, mystery shopping, and talking to my counterparts at other companies. Of course, I also observed how to avoid the missteps that others made.

I have also experienced how competing salespeople or firms can cooperate for the benefit of their customers. For example, numerous lenders have referred me loans that they considered too difficult to handle. I would not hesitate to do the same if we were in a similar situation. In addition, loan originators at other firms often call me to ask for advice on marketing or related topics and I am always willing to share a few details about our non-proprietary programs.

Having a positive working relationship with competitors can pay unexpected dividends. Among the financial services firms Gold Star competed against for several years was a good size mortgage banker whose management style I highly respected. They were very professional and in many ways ran their business like we did. One day the branch manager of this nationwide firm called me to arrange a meeting. He came to my office and we shared a few stories before he got to the point. He was tired of managing a large group of salespeople and support staff during a very challenging market, although unlike some other mortgage bankers, he had been quite successful. He leaned forward and said simply, "I want to get back to originating and think this would be a good fit." He even offered to bring some of his top salespeople along. This former sales manager subsequently joined us and has been a top producer ever since. Such an arrangement likely would not have been possible if we had an adversarial relationship.

Don't Criticize Them

As tempting as it may seem at times, salespeople should never criticize their competitors, at least not in an overt manner. It's too easy to complain to a customer that the other salesperson "doesn't know what they are doing," "is not ethical," or "uses bait and switch tactics." The problem with being noticeably critical of other salespeople is that customers and prospects may view you as being defensive, unsure of yourself and generally unprofessional. There are ways to point out a competitor's deficiencies in a more subtle manner. For example, when a prospect tells me about another firm that I believe is making outrageous claims or otherwise engaged in questionable practices, I will usually advise her to check for possible complaints with the Better Business Bureau, government agency or the Internet, and to be wary of excessive promises.

I have also found that sometimes your "best" critics can end up working for you. I had an interesting experience that illustrates both the power of "karma" and the importance of having a thick skin when it comes to criticism. I was interviewing an experienced loan officer candidate who had run his own mortgage company for 28 years, but had to close it because of the lending industry crisis. We talked for a few minutes, reviewed his background and then he made a surprising confession. "When you started your first company, I was a big critic of yours because you were young and I saw you as a competitor," he said, obviously embarrassed. "I started rumors that you didn't have the best rates and that your claim for fast turnaround was false. During the last 10 years, I've watched as you gained market share and moved to larger offices." He turned away for a few seconds, then looked straight at me and shook his head. "I apologize for criticizing you like that." I could tell he was contrite. "Now, here I am asking you for a job...and I couldn't think of a better place to be," he added. How interesting, I thought, that a former competitor was admitting to publicly criticizing me, about which I had not been aware. I hesitated briefly, knowing that it would be easy to turn him away at that point. However, he seemed to be the best candidate for the job and I was more concerned with continuing to build a strong company than reacting negatively to a previous slight. I smiled and reached out to shake his hand. "Congratulations and welcome to Gold Star," I said. That was a great decision; he has been one of our best salespeople.

Maintain Perspective

Having a better understanding of how the competition performs will help you refine your own overall sales strategies. I believe that mystery shopping and other techniques can be valuable parts of a salesperson's ongoing education. However, it is a matter of balance.

Some salespeople do get overly consumed with the competition and lose sight of what they should be doing to develop their own programs. I am convinced that one of the reasons certain companies imploded during the lending industry's meltdown was their emphasis on reacting to what competitors were doing, rather than concentrating on what was best for their own organization. For example, many firms saw others get rich from the subprime bonanza and rushed to cash in by creating similar products. They were intent on chasing other bankers' short-term successes, rather than being true to their own original business plans.

While we do spend time in sales meetings and other company discussions reviewing competitor strengths and weaknesses, this is a small percentage of our daily and weekly activity. We generally don't react to a competitor's product or pricing strategies by significantly changing Gold Star's business practices or otherwise altering our long-term plans. One of the significant signs that a salesperson or company CEO has matured is when they know not to be overly concerned about a competitor's successes, or waste much time gloating about a competitor's difficulties.

I must admit, though, that I never get tired of hearing that we're one of the best in the nation.

Chapter Ten
Making Your Net Work

"The successful networkers I know, the ones receiving tons of referrals and feeling truly happy about themselves, continually put the other person's needs ahead of their own."

~Bob Burg

B USINESS CARDS ARE a waste of time. I will clarify that rather bold statement. I believe that business cards are overrated as an effective networking tool. Salespeople (and others) typically hand out their cards at every opportunity—social functions, business meetings, golf courses and grocery stores—expecting that recipients will add them to their database as a reminder to call with referrals. Salespeople have used a wide variety of creative approaches to attract attention, including jumbo size cards and video cards. Of course, some business cards are discarded right away, others are put in a desk drawer or Rolodex file, and a few are kept for more immediate attention.

The salesperson introduction/referral request letter is another overrated, and potentially abused, networking strategy. New salespeople typically send them to relatives, high school and college classmates, former neighbors, barber, dentist, and everyone else as a way to generate immediate business. The problem with this approach is that many prospective clients don't want to be the novice salesperson's first sale. Perhaps she has just graduated from college and is now an insurance company trainee. Or he has been working as a teacher and switched to real estate. In many cases, their various network contacts would prefer they had some experience. In several instances a relative has actually asked me, rather than their niece or nephew, to handle a home purchase. Of course, once the originator was established, they could gain their relative's future business.

The point is that you have to build your network carefully; it is not an overnight process. There is definitely a place for business cards and the introduction letter in your overall networking strategy, but you need to be selective and make sure the timing is right.

The 250 Formula

The ideal network is a group of prime professional and personal contacts who will enthusiastically recommend your services to others. A network database should be highly organized, with the latest details of the customer's last purchase, future plans, job information and so on.

Many salespeople rely on the well-known 250 formula, which was based on the original theory that about 250 people attend most weddings and funerals and therefore that most of us know approximately 250 people who each represent a source of business. It's hard to argue with the basic math, although the magic number might be closer to 125 or 200 depending on the popularity of the brides and grooms you know.

Salespeople typically create a network list of everyone they have ever known, without being overly concerned whether the prospects are able to afford major purchases. When I was starting out, I didn't have the connections that many of the better-established loan officers did. I figured the more people I talked to, the larger my network would grow. I learned an essential ingredient for creating an effective network is a master list that can be broken into subgroups, such as primary partners, secondary influencers and others. While I lacked the experience of many more seasoned loan originators in my market, I did recognize a fact that most of them hadn't yet accepted: it really is better to give than to receive, at least until you have developed strong relationships with your network partners. It is about providing something of value.

CARDS & DOUGHNUTS

When I first got into the mortgage business I wanted to develop referral sources. I was told by experienced mortgage officers to build relationships with real estate agents. What I figured out was that in most cases, experience meant time in the business and not necessarily production. Being new to the business, I asked how to proceed. I was told to take a box of doughnuts or bagels to the office and drop them off with business cards. It did not take long to figure out that they were eating the treats and tossing the cards, as I wasn't receiving any calls. So I came up with an idea to call and find out when they were holding their weekly or monthly meeting. I asked if I could come by and bring some bagels or doughnuts and introduce myself. At least half the time I was welcomed. So when I came to the meetings I would put an empty doughnut box on the table and start my speech. "Good morning folks. What I have today is information to help grow your business," I explained. At this time, I would open the box and pass it around. At first I'm sure there was some disappointment, but as soon as I gave them some great information they were hooked. At the end of the meeting I would close with. "I hope the information was beneficial and I do have doughnuts for you now." This usually received a good laugh and helped to build strong relationships. It just shows that there are different ways to start your network.

—Michael Hyman, Gold Star

Providing Value

Most salespeople are inclined to ask for referrals (some more aggressively than others) without first having something to offer in return. However, that generally doesn't generate the same level of long-term results. Early on, I discovered that the key was to become indispensable to other business professionals by helping them in some way, before asking for their assistance with my goals. This was largely based on my sincere commitment to help them succeed, and on knowing that it was a good way to develop my own mortgage business. I realized that most of my competitors were following the traditional route—sending interest rate sheets to Realtors and asking them for referrals. I also saw that real estate agents often treated such originators as doormats, which I had no desire to be.

I devised a simple way to establish a positive rapport with real estate agents and get past the gatekeeper, the receptionist who often guarded the access of their offices. I pre-qualified several borrowers who were serious about purchasing a home. I then visited a major Realtor's office and explained to the receptionist, "I am interested in buying a house and wanted to see if there is an agent able to help me." Of course, there was an agent anxious to assist a prospective homebuyer. When the agent met me in the waiting area, I smiled and quickly said, "My name is Dan, I am a loan officer and actually I represent a pre-qualified borrower who is eager to find a home in the area and should be a good client for you. Are you taking any new clients?" I figured the offer of a good client would likely outweigh my slight deception. I remember the agent looking at me with uncertainty; she obviously had not encountered many originators who brought her a prospect so soon in the relationship. From my perspective, it was the ideal way to immediately overcome the typical objection that "I'm sorry, I already have longstanding relationships with several other loan originators and don't need another one now." How could she object if I was handing her a client?

Of course, the agent was accepting new clients. "Yes, I am sure I can help," she replied. Then I called the borrower, handed my phone to the agent and encouraged her to make the necessary house hunting arrangements with the new client. Afterwards, we talked for a few minutes and I said that I would call her again soon. Much to the agent's surprise, I didn't say a word about referrals. During the next week, I met with agents at nine other major Realtor offices, presenting each one with an interested buyer, but asking no one for referrals. About two weeks later, I called the agents to ask how the discussions with the new clients were progressing and to make arrangements to stop by and provide another pre-qualified borrower. At this point, I had given each agent two solid referrals in a month without asking for anything in return, and then made another offer they found difficult to refuse. "Hopefully these referrals have been productive for you," I said on my return visit. "I would also like to call the new people on your open house sign-up sheets and emphasize what a great Realtor you are." Of course, a few of them thought that I had ulterior motives, but eventually they all thought this was a wonderful idea and that I was sincerely interested in helping them grow their business, which I was.

We later developed another network enhancing technique— offering to be Realtors' back-up telemarketers. We suggested that we could help follow up on the Website queries they had not had time to answer. Our telemarketers would call the agents' prospects and say: "I am calling on behalf of Happy Homes Realtors and understand you are looking for a house. Are you still in the market?" Then we would gather the appropriate information to share with the agent. It was a special value added benefit that no one else was providing them.

We would eventually emphasize our interest in receiving their referrals, but now we could do so more from a position of strength, as true network partners. We also didn't need to stress our willingness to handle their especially difficult transactions, which some originators do as a way to get established with agents. The risk with this approach is that you can get the reputation for handling only the problem sales that others don't want. In addition, you may not be able to salvage the sale and then become a failure in the agent's eyes. However, over time we have gained a reputation for doing the more challenging deals as well.

It didn't take long for the 10 real estate agents to call with referrals and introduce me to other top agents in their office, and as a result we were receiving referrals on a steady basis. I knew this value-first approach wasn't a new strategy, but to my knowledge no one else in my market was doing it.

One of our salespeople has used a simpler, but very effective way to make a connection with Realtors. "When talking to my Realtors both old and new I try and make small talk and find out what they are interested in, what their hobbies are and what makes them tick," he explained. Once he finds out what their interests are, he goes online to cheapmagazines.com to find a magazine that pertains to their hobby and purchases a one-year subscription, which costs an average $10 per year. "When I fill out the subscription form, I put my name first, then the Realtor's info, so every month when they get the magazine it has my name on the cover. At least once a month they think of me and the gift that I have given them."

FIVE GOLDEN NETWORKING RULES

1. *Provide value first, then ask for referrals.*
2. *Don't rely on business cards or flyers as a primary networking strategy.*
3. *Combine novice salespeople with experienced in your master network.*
4. *Monitor the success of your network.*
5. *Incorporate social media strategies.*

Expanding The Network

I gradually expanded my professional network to include attorneys, financial planners, major sports celebrities and their agents, and others. For example, we always ask our clients if they have a will or trust and if not, call the appropriate estate-planning attorney and refer them. When clients are in the process of a divorce, we have the opportunity to contact a divorce attorney with referrals of clients needing assistance. This simple concept of providing value before asking for referrals can easily be adapted to most areas of sales. You just have to find out how to best help your network partners enhance their business. In addition to providing referrals, you may be able to help refine their business plan, survey their customers, or do joint marketing.

I believe a network is enhanced with the inclusion of people of various experience levels. Many salespeople argue that the best way to create an effective network is by working with the top producers in their respective fields, such as the most experienced CPAs, Realtors, attorneys, sports agents and technology consultants. Why waste time with those who haven't yet established themselves? That seems to make sense, but it is actually a shortsighted notion, because many of the newer ones will eventually become successful and you have an opportunity to grow with them.

You have to continually evaluate prospects as if they had just been drafted by a sports team; determine which have the potential of long-term success and then provide the necessary support.

NEW CENTERS OF INFLUENCE

One of the easiest strategies to add centers of influence (a professional who works with the clientele you want to work with) to your network is seeking the cooperation of your customer contacts. I know a financial services advisor who uses the following proven technique:

"After the client mentions she works with a center of influence (COI) she trusts (CPA, attorney etc.), I ask for permission and then call the professional to introduce myself:

" *Mr. COI, we have a common client. He spoke highly of you. Some of my clients may have a need for your services, so I'd like to learn more about your business and see if there might be a good fit."*

If the COI is receptive, I continue:

"Plus, I'm hoping there might be some ways we could help each other out in our businesses. Let's get together for a cup of coffee/lunch)?"

During the meeting I focus on the COI's needs. I always try to find out as much as possible about his business. It's almost like qualifying a prospect. Here are some of the questions I would normally ask:

" *How did you get started in the business?"*

"Where do you get most of your business?"

" *What kind of business are you looking for? Who is your ideal client?"*

"Whom do you typically refer business to?"

"Do you have other advisers that you are currently referring business to? How is that going?"

"What can I do for you? How can I help your business?"

Once I determined that the COI is a good fit and receptive, I bring up the topic of referrals in a pretty straightforward manner:

"I am looking for a resource in your industry (town/county) to recommend my professional contacts and also, ideally, I'm looking for someone who is open to recommending me to the people they know."

Earlier in my career, I would sponsor some educational seminars for my clients and prospects. I would ask a COI to be a speaker at the event on the subject of his expertise. I would encourage him to invite his clients as well. This way, both of us would get an introduction to possible prospects.

For example, I met a former ice hockey player who retired and became a life insurance agent. He needed help getting established in this competitive field. I explained that I would introduce him to clients needing insurance as well as financial planners and others who might need his service. I wanted to help him get started as others had provided support to me. He has continued to excel and we have developed a mutually beneficial relationship.

Group Action

I have never been a big supporter of formal networking groups that meet on a weekly basis and whose members share leads with each other. I know that many business professionals think they are a sure method of developing referrals and that's fine if it works for them. Because of the pressure to provide referrals, they are often given without a great deal of thought and tend to be unqualified, so the meetings could be a waste of time. I am certainly not denigrating the overall effectiveness of such groups. The challenge is to be certain that the leads you do receive are worthwhile and that membership in a particular group helps you continue to expand your business.

I also know several salespeople who have formed their own, more informal network associations. One extremely successful salesperson joined a group that seemed to offer several advantages. "The group I belong to includes an attorney, CPA, real estate agent, insurance agent and a financial planner," he said. "We meet informally, two or three times a year, usually for lunch. Most of the lunch is fun time, with a bit of business. We exchange information concerning what is happening in each of our areas of knowledge and expertise. We all use each other's services, and continue to refer clients to each other. This network group has been ongoing for at least eight years." The benefits are obvious. "Not only is there an exchange of tangible business clients, but if I need a tax question answered, I can always count on a timely response from my tax contact, or for a legal question, I will get a direct line to my attorney without waiting. The other benefit is that each of us has contacts with other people, such as contractors, plumbers, or repair people that can complement our business, and enable each of us to help our client base when requested. When I close a loan, I hand my client a group of business cards from this informal group and explain how I know this group of professionals will help if they need their service. I call this my Trust Group. It works and my borrowers have commented on what a great idea it is."

Another sales colleague took an even more proactive approach by creating his own networking group. "I solicited different trade people along with other professionals whose services I had used or was using and told them that I was forming a group of 'Proven Professionals' looking to see if they would be interested in participating," he told me. "I said that they needed to provide me with 200 business cards and share in the expense ($50.00) of getting this off the ground. They would also need to provide stellar service at an affordable price to anyone who contacted them. I then ordered 500 card caddies embossed with my name, company name and cell phone number. I loaded 45 caddies with a card from each profession, mine being first (in the same order), and scheduled an evening of cocktails and hors d'oeuvres, with attendance being mandatory. I had my assistant greet everyone as they arrived at the restaurant, whose owner was one of the participants. After all of the participants had arrived, I requested everyone's attention and I explained what would be happening. I gave a five-minute introduction/ bio followed by each person in the book and strongly encouraged that each participant make a concerted effort to refer each other. I also explained that I would be handing out one of these at each of my sales; explaining to my clients that these were my "preferred" vendors and that I had personally used each and every one of them at one time or another. There was electricity in the air and the program proved to be very successful."

When considering the benefits of group involvement, look beyond your immediate industry. My brother Alex, a highly successful Realtor, has found an effective way to expand his network by participating on the board of directors of several high-profile nonprofit organizations. "This gives me the opportunity to become an 'in-house' Realtor for that group and its members," he noted.

Refining Your Network

Obviously, you can't let your network get stale. It's important to continue monitoring the effectiveness so that it produces the results you anticipate. On a regular basis you should analyze the primary criteria you have established, such as an increase in referrals and closed sales. When was the last time you referred deals to each other? Have you talked with them recently? What can you do to enhance the relationship?

Of course, the networking process has evolved during the last decade, with social media techniques having a major impact on the way salespeople market. For example, there is no question that Facebook and LinkedIn have helped many substantially expand and enhance their network. An increasing number of salespeople at Gold Star and other organizations of which I am aware, have a separate Facebook page solely for business. They use it as a primary way to connect with their customers, and provide product, company and industry information. While younger salespeople may seem to be more comfortable with social media techniques—because they grew up in the "Internet age"—all salespeople need to adapt to this newer networking strategy.

Some salespeople remind us that the most basic networking strategies are still quite effective. "The best way I know is the good old-fashioned 'smile and dial,' monthly calls to five people you have not talked to in the past 90-120 days," a longtime salesman told me. "Networking by picking up the phone and making the call always goes a long way. Maybe you end up scheduling a meeting with a past customer who just started a new company, or an old colleague who can share tips and useful information on your competition. Either way, it is what I find to be the best. There are many ways to network these days, but for me, nothing beats doing it the old-fashioned way. I set reminders in my calendar each month for five folks I want to reach out to that I haven't spoken with or seen in quite a while."

Chapter Eleven
Forty Ways to Ruin a Sale...and How to Avoid Them

"Success seems to be connected with action. Successful people keep moving. They make mistakes, but they don't quit."
~Conrad Hilton

AS I WAS WRITING *The ABC of Sales*, I had an opportunity to talk with a group of salespeople from different professions. We began thinking about the common errors that salespeople make, some of which aren't covered elsewhere in the book, and others are worth repeating in a new context. It was an interesting, rewarding opportunity to watch successful people from different backgrounds and experience levels mention some of the "errors" they have committed and how they can easily be rectified.

For instance, Al Wootton, a longtime mortgage industry veteran, recalled his first day on the job as an account executive. "The territory was wide open, and I could call on any accounts I wanted," he said. "I put together a target list and since I was a new guy, I was afraid to go after the larger, big name accounts. About four months later, I was at the yearly mortgage broker expo where lenders and the existing customer base came to display products and learn who and what was available. A gentleman walked up to my booth and began looking at our handouts and talking to me about the product. Further into the discussion, we determined our offices were about a mile from each other and that I had been there for a while. He was a large name player that I was a little intimidated by and I had been waiting to call him until I felt I was good enough to win his business. Then came his question: 'Why haven't you called me yet?' he asked. I nearly fell down. He wanted to hear from me and was surprised that he hadn't. I had driven by his office almost every day for months and had thought several times that I would one day become an established salesman that he wanted to hear from. I learned the hard way that he was surprised that I hadn't taken a shot and he wasn't impressed. I learned after that to pick up the phone and dial it, because the risk of not calling was worse than the fear of failure."

Of course, Al has long since learned the importance of not being intimidated and failing to contact what new salespeople often perceive as the "larger prospects." In addition to his Top 40 mistake, I received a variety of other suggestions. We agreed that while some of them may seem elementary, we can all benefit from an occasional tutorial. As Al noted, "Remembering all of these sales experiences and the lessons learned has been rewarding. It's awesome to remember how exciting it was when I first started selling."

So, in addition to Al's contribution, here are another 39 frequent sales mistakes (in no order of importance) and a few ideas to avoid them. In fact, many of them could be applied to various non-sales aspects of our lives.

1. *Being embarrassed to be a salesman.* During the last several years, many salespeople have sought new titles to describe their profession, such as advisor or consultant. Some do it as part of their overall marketing strategy, to distinguish themselves from the competition. However, others believe that a different title somehow adds more credibility to what they perceive as a slightly tarnished profession. You cannot ignore the fact that you are a salesperson. You sell products and services. It is an honorable profession.

2. *Poor follow-up.* You don't have time to call the customer to see how your product or service has performed. Then why should the customer subsequently care about your interest in repeat business or referrals? It does not take much effort to make a phone call or send an e-mail to see how they're enjoying their purchase and if they have any questions or suggestions.

3. *Not qualifying prospects.* While you do not want to ignore people who at first glance may appear to be marginal prospects (see # 18), you also don't want to spend too much time with those who don't intend to or are unable to buy. By doing basic homework, you should be able to confirm whether they are a bona fide customer. If in doubt, consider them a good prospect.

4. *Over-promising/ under-delivering.* Every salesperson is taught this essential maxim, but many forget it as they try to excite the customer by pledging an early delivery date or making other special promises. Customers are always impressed when you under-promise and then provide exceptional results. It is always better to be conservative in your offering.

5. *Improperly setting expectations.* Closely related to the preceding error. You need to advise the customer upfront what to expect regarding the cost, accessory options, guarantees and availability. Do it in writing and if necessary review in person. There should be no surprises.

6. *Not having sufficient understanding of clients' personalities.* Obviously, there is no single customer type. Some are patient, appreciative and friendly; others are impatient, abrupt and ungrateful. Customers have differing desires, concerns and frustrations. Everybody doesn't respond to the same sales presentation, so you must try to adapt your approach to meet the varying personality types. You don't have to be an expert in psychology, but it helps to have at least a basic understanding of customer profiling.

7. *Forgetting names.* Everyone appreciates being remembered. Some salespeople have a "photographic memory;" others take longer to recall prospect or business partner names. You can be excused for forgetting someone's name during the first meeting; after that it may appear that you just don't care. Use whatever memory system you can to improve your recall.

8. *Missing the details.* As the well-known phrase suggests: "The devil is in the details." That is where so many transactions break down. You forget to have one minor form signed, neglect to inform the customer of the return policy or overlook some other small, but

crucial item. If you continue to miss such details, it's time to create a "cheat sheet," "Sales Detail Inventory" or other reminder to ensure you check off every possible requirement.

9. *Not walking away when the customer "fit" is not right.* Even the most aggressive, stubborn salesperson knows that not every prospect should become a customer. Perhaps they want a product that you can't provide or seek unreasonable terms. Maybe they are too difficult to work with. Do everything you can to please a prospect, but know when to walk away. Explain that you don't have what they are looking for and refer them to someone else.

10. *Difficulty handling rejection.* If you cannot deal with rejection, you should not be in sales. Salespeople are often rejected by prospects and others. There are days when it seems you can't sell anything. You do not have to be insensitive, but salespeople do need moderately thick skin. Don't take rejection personally…unless there is a reason to. (You have made a major error that led to the unwanted rejection.)

11. *Not listening, interrupting.* Customers consider this one of the worst offenses. They have just begun to explain what they want, and you cut in to share your wisdom. They will forgive you the first time you interrupt them, but when there is a pattern of inattention, they will likely realize that you really aren't listening. And if you are not listening, you must not understand their situation. So listen carefully to what your prospect is saying. Give them a chance to finish their sentence (or paragraph), rather than always thinking about what you want to say next.

12. *Thinking of only your self-interest, not giving back to the community.* You are not required to donate your time and money to worthwhile causes, but it certainly helps. It is the right thing to do and also helps strengthen your ties with business partners. There are so many ways to show your enthusiasm for helping others, many of which don't require much time or money. Work with others at your company or at another firm to raise funds or contribute in other ways.

13.*Not making yourself indispensable to customers.* Your customers should feel that they cannot live without you and your product or service. You accomplish this by providing the best product at a reasonable price, in addition to offering the more intangible benefits. The latter includes thinking of their interests first, being available and responding promptly to their queries. The goal is to have them always think of you when they are considering another purchase.

14. *Being complacent.* Even the best salespeople need to avoid being overly content. Complacency often occurs when you ignore the competition or take your customers for granted, and believe that you know everything about sales and your industry. You stop paying attention to some of the most critical areas. Never stop learning, improving your skills and seeking new opportunities to enhance your customer relations.

15. *Not realizing when the customer has agreed to the purchase (overselling).* There is always a certain point in the sales process when the prospect is ready to buy. They are convinced you have the best product and are ready to write a check. At this point, some salespeople continue selling, not realizing that their audience may find a reason to cancel the sale. For example, you may unconsciously raise a new issue that the customer had not considered, or she may think you are too pushy and begin to reconsider the purchase. Stop selling when you see the obvious signs, such as the customer nodding his head or holding her checkbook.

16. *Not doing basic research on potential or existing clients before meeting with them.* I have talked to a number of job candidates who did not know even the most basic facts about our company. All they needed to do was visit the Gold Star website. All salespeople should conduct their own research before meeting with any business partner. Learn enough from their Website, news articles, Chamber of Commerce or other source so that you can demonstrate your interest in making them your employer or client.

17. *Giving final ultimatums or having a "take-it-or-leave-it" attitude.* None of us enjoys being backed into a corner, forced to make a quick decision. Most prospects do not like hearing "If you don't buy now, you won't be able to get the same model..." or "You'll not get the same deal if you wait until tomorrow." Of course, if you need to mention any legitimate time constraint—such as a changing interest

rate or special sales price—give them an objective explanation along with the appropriate options, but don't make unnecessary ultimatums.

18. *Assuming the prospect isn't able to afford a product or service based on their appearance or demeanor.* You are "judging the book by its cover." The obvious example of this is when a casually dressed patron enters a high-end jewelry store or car showroom. The salesman takes a quick look and decides that the prospect cannot afford to make a purchase. They carry on a hurried conversation and the salesperson asks an assistant to take over, prompting the prospect to go elsewhere to make a large purchase. Treat everyone equally until you are certain they are not a legitimate customer.

19. *Being impatient with clients who need extra attention and explanation.* Customers can easily tell that their salesperson is irritated when they have too many questions or ask to have points repeated. When they sense that irritation in your voice, the customer may become defensive and tune you out. Spend whatever time it takes to satisfy the prospect's questions and concerns. Some people require more "hand holding" than others.

20. *Giving the impression you are doing the customer a "favor" by providing the service.* This may be evident by a condescending attitude, underwhelming customer service or other behavior that conveys you are in control and the customer is "merely" paying for the product. You cannot forget that without customers, there is no business. Customers must know that you appreciate them.

21. *Dressing inappropriately.* You would think everyone should know the importance of following proper dress (and hygiene) guidelines. Anyone who meets and greets the public—as a salesman or any other profession—should wear appropriate attire. So if you are trying to impress a prospect, dressing casually (jeans, polo shirt, shorts) probably doesn't work. This doesn't mean you have to wear designer outfits and expensive suits. You do have to dress for the occasion.

22. *Using technical terms that clients don't understand.* Customers usually do not like it when they have to ask you to explain various terms. Assume that they don't understand the intricacies of your

industry. Think of "prospect friendly" alternatives to industry jargon. You don't have to "dumb down" your presentation to make it understandable, just minimize the more complex wording.

23. *Accepting "no" for an answer, when you detect "waffling."* Sometimes salespeople give up just a little too easily. Customers often want you to give them additional assurances that they are making the right decision. They may not mean "no," but rather "I need to be convinced that this is the right decision." Before accepting "no," try a few additional questions or suggestions to get a positive response.

24. *Failing to track your marketing and sales efforts on a daily basis.* It is essential to know where customers heard about you and what marketing activities are most effective. At the very least you should ask customers what prompted them to call you and keep an ongoing log that details the source of referrals and other contacts.

25. *Being scared to tell someone you don't know.* Of course, customers appreciate the most knowledgeable salespeople, those who have answers to nearly every question. However, they also understand when you don't have an immediate response. When you don't know, just say "That's a good question, allow me to look into it and get right back to you."

26. *Not taking care of the smaller customers because you only want the big ones.* It is easy to dismiss prospects that don't seem to have larger budgets and that you don't believe have the potential of being a major account. However, most of us have examples of smaller customers who have grown into bigger ones or referred you to a larger account. Evaluate long-term customer potential, not just the short-term gain.

27. *Letting pride get in the way.* Pride can keep you from asking someone for help or give a referral to another salesperson because they may be better equipped to deal with it. Before letting this occur, always ask: "What's best for the customer and the company?" If it means having someone else handle a sale, that's probably the best action. Doing so will generally improve your rapport and reputation with everyone involved.

28. *Not respecting their opinions.* The salesperson should be the expert in his/her field. However, customers have their own opinions and they will usually want to share them with you. Let customers express their thoughts as to the product or service best suited to their needs, even if you believe they are completely wrong. They will most likely end up agreeing with you and meanwhile will appreciate that you have listened to their opinion.

29. *Not validating their fears and concerns.* Customers are often worried whether it's the right product, if they really need it and so on. The more expensive the purchase, the greater their concerns. It is essential that salespeople accept these issues as valid and help customers feel comfortable with the sale. Compliment them on their choice, emphasize that it is a long-term investment and that they have received a good deal.

30. *Difficulty losing gracefully.* No one likes to lose a sale to a competitor, at your own or another company. But it happens. Ideally, you will have greater overall success than the other salespeople. Learn why you lost the sale to avoid a repeat performance, and then move on to the next opportunities. Complaining about a lost sale won't enhance your image within the company or with customers.

31. *Not letting customers know that they are more important than your commission check.* Customers are well aware that you depend on sales and referrals. But they also want to know you have their best interests in mind. They want to believe that you consider them a loyal customer and even a friend. Whenever possible, acknowledge customers as being important to your professional (and personal) welfare.

32. *Not being aware that clients are not only buying a product but they are buying (testing) you.* Most people are potential repeat customers, in the process of finding an ongoing source for their products or services. They are looking for a salesperson they can trust and relate to, and your total performance can cement or impede the relationship. Remember, you may make that first or second sale to a customer but end up losing them as a "customer for life." Use all available techniques to make a solid first impression,

impress them throughout the transaction and then maintain the appropriate follow-up.

33. *Changing your tone of voice when a client gets irritated.* Altering your voice when the prospect seems upset or confused would seem like a normal reaction. However, if you raise your voice, it could make the client even more irritable or frustrated. You should always be the "voice of reason." Strive to talk them back to a calmer attitude and then address any situation that initially may have set them off.

34. *Looking at your phone, not the customer.* It is a difficult habit to break: checking your phone and sending text messages during meetings. While that may be tolerated (even encouraged in certain circumstances) with your peers during a company sales meeting, you do not want to alienate clients or business partners. It tends to make them think you are not paying attention, which, of course, you aren't. So wait until after your client meeting to check your phone or BlackBerry.

35. *Not properly scheduling meetings.* If you aren't careful, meetings can consume your time. It is essential that you actually schedule them with a set length, whether they are with a client or someone else. Then, remind the participants of the allotted time and subject matter: "Hello Tom. Thanks for taking 15 minutes to meet with me today. What I'd like to do is discuss the pricing issues and me using your condo in Florida every other weekend. Sound good?" By doing this you won't irritate the client by holding the meeting to l5 minutes when they had anticipated it would be longer. Of course, you still have the option of extending the meeting for a few minutes.

36. *Failing to ask for advice from senior/more experienced colleagues.* Most salespeople work with one or more highly experienced colleagues. They are a great resource on dealing with difficult customers, marketing techniques, sales reports and a variety of other topics. Some salespeople do not take advantage of this resource, because they prefer to do everything on their own or for some other reason. Why not ask for pointers on a few areas that you find especially challenging? You might learn something, and will undoubtedly strengthen the rapport with your peers.

37. *Neglecting to ask for referrals throughout the sales process.* Yes, you ask for the referral once you have completed the sale, but what about all the other opportunities? For example, why not mention your interest in referrals the first time you meet a prospect ("I am glad I was able to answer your initial questions and look forward to discussing next steps tomorrow. By the way, be sure to mention my name to your friends or work associates who may be looking for a new car, home loan, life insurance, etc.")? Depending on the length of the sales transaction, there are other good times to ask for referrals. Clients generally won't mind how many times you ask, as long as you do so in a non-aggressive manner.

38. *Not learning from other industries.* It is easy to become insulated, to concentrate solely on your own industry. However, you may be neglecting your overall sales education. You can gain valuable insights about sales challenges, marketing techniques and much more from other professions. If you sell or lease cars, you can study how top salespeople in real estate, mortgage lending and furniture approach their business. Loan originators can learn how salespeople in insurance, financial planning, and other professions market their services. Spend an hour or two each week educating yourself about selling in other industries.

39. *Taking yourself way too seriously.* Most salespeople provide a valuable service or product, the kind on which many consumers depend, on either a short- or long-term basis. However, we are not curing a disease or teaching young people to become productive citizens. It is good to keep everything in perspective. When you get frustrated because a customer "just doesn't understand how important this policy is," or "ought to be able to understand why our XYZ product is much better than the competitor's inferior model," remember that it isn't the end of the world or a negative blot on your reputation if they don't buy from you that day, or at all. There will be another day, another customer and many more opportunities in the future.

Chapter Twelve
The Past and Future Salesperson

"The best way to predict the future is to create it."
~Peter Drucker

I t is hard to believe that not so long ago, most salespeople actually took all customer applications by hand, or that consumers could only buy books, shoes and computers at retail outlets. So much has changed in the sales profession, and there is so much to look forward to that I envy salespeople of the future. They will be better trained, have amazing opportunities and enjoy more respect than their predecessors.

I have a good understanding of the future of Gold Star, but am also interested in the future of the sales profession and, more specifically, the challenges and opportunities that await salespeople in different fields. For newer salespeople and those who haven't yet started their sales careers, these potential developments should be of special interest.

Evolution of Sales

The sales function has substantially evolved during the last 50+ years, since pioneering salespeople began "peddling" cash registers, encyclopedias, cars and a myriad of other products. Early salespeople often carried bulky sample cases door-to-door. Now it's the age of the Internet marketplace.

The dramatic changes to the sales profession have greatly affected the way we conduct business. For example, as late as 1998 loan officers took handwritten applications, careful not to make a mistake because "white out" or correction tape was not allowed (to avoid the appearance of fraud). The automated approval process hadn't been developed. Overworked appraisers would prepare their handwritten reports and attach a Polaroid photo, hoping that one day electronic submissions would make their jobs easier. It typically took an agonizingly slow 90 days to close a loan. Taking applications on an office computer, a laptop or more recently an iPad has significantly streamlined the loan process. A borrower with good credit can have their loan closed in 15 days, even in today's stricter lending environment.

Salespeople in other professions have experienced similar changes. Whereas earlier it was necessary to conduct most business face-to-face, e-mail has offered a faster way to initiate contact and provide status reports. A proliferation of software programs has enhanced much of the salesperson's daily routine, from the initial application process to database management.

Online sales have increased in diverse product categories. Dell Computers was one of the first companies to embrace Internet commerce; eventually followed by Amazon.com, Zappos.com and numerous others. Much of the change in the way people buy is dictated by shifting demographics; the younger generation is more comfortable with Internet stores, preferring to make many purchases from their favorite Websites.

There may be a few long-time salespeople who prefer the pre-Internet era, but I have yet to meet any of them.

Looking Ahead

Other than predicting that subprime loans would eventually create havoc with mortgage lending and the nation's economy, and to make regular forecasts for Gold Star's sales volume and related statistics, I have avoided making generalized conclusions about the future. Armchair prognosticating is a risky pastime; too many predictions are off the mark and even the wisest experts make major mistakes. However, I have become fascinated with the evolution of the sales profession and the varied changes that we can anticipate in the next 10-20 years.

Following are my observations, based on experience, discussions with other successful salespeople and, of course, some creative thinking.

- **Expanded Opportunities**—There definitely will be a wider variety and a greater number of opportunities for salespeople. An increase in products and services across all industries will mean more sales career choices. Product offerings will become even more refined as new product development in auto manufacturing, consumer finance, insurance, electronics and other industries becomes increasingly sophisticated and aggressive in meeting customer demands.

- **A Virtual Sales Force**—One of the most interesting developments will be a more extensive use of the virtual sales force. Various industries already have part- or full-time salespeople working from "home" offices, and this will be even more prevalent in the near future. More companies will see the wisdom of minimizing the "brick and mortar" expenses of adding new office space, and instead have salespeople work from home offices networked to headquarters, with all of the appropriate support.

  As this book was being published (May 2011), Gold Star was about to introduce its own Virtual Loan Officer Platform. Our plans included adding a number of experienced loan officers who would work from their own offices and receive the full range of Gold Star's extensive support services. In addition to eliminating the need to open a series of new offices in key markets, we are taking advantage of the availability of many veteran originators, including some who are semi-retired and want to work on their own production schedule. The Virtual Sales Force concept will eventually be adopted by many other industries.

- **Better Educated Salespeople**—We will see an even greater emphasis on education to prepare people for a sales career.

There will still be on-the-job training, but it will be much more formal and comprehensive as companies upgrade their trainee and mentoring programs to match their competitors' advanced curricula.

In addition, more colleges and universities will create professional selling programs, such as the one developed by Baylor University. I envision more high level internships, enabling students to gain valuable experience at top flight companies. There will also be more continuing education requirements to keep pace with industry developments and diverse options to meet them.

Ideally, more successful salespeople will add their expertise as classroom instructors, partially dispelling the tired phrase "Those who can't do, teach."

• **Technology to Advance, Streamline**—Technological advancements will continue at near warp speed and have a major impact on the sales function. In addition to the virtual sales force, we will see technology take an even more critical role in the way we develop leads, interact with customers, process and close the sale, and establish brand awareness on a more global basis.

While I hesitate to pinpoint specific tech advancements, I am intrigued about the potential that tablet computers will have in expanding business with customers and strategic partners. In addition, Facebook pages, personal Websites, smart phone applications and Twitter accounts may be surpassed as the most effective tools for salespeople.

Salespeople of the future will be more attuned to technological applications generally and within their specific profession. Our own hiring criteria emphasizes the importance of having a high technology I.Q. and I am aware of a number of companies that have a similar preference. The most successful salespeople will be computer and tech savvy and work with IT consultants to ensure that they are on the cutting edge of sales-related technology.

- **Pursuit of Sales Knowledge**—Salespeople will need to be more knowledgeable about their industry, products, and marketing techniques. Those who sell computers, phones, cars and other feature-rich products may find it especially challenging to master the complex data sheets, technical bulletins and other information and effortlessly explain them to customers. Consumers are more educated as to their options, and salespeople must be able to demonstrate they have the answers. Salespeople will have a better grasp of demographics than their predecessors, studying buying patterns, shifting populations and other topics.

  In addition to reading the many available sales books and attending their industry conferences, salespeople will share information with each other via blogs and video conferencing. At Gold Star, we frequently provide salespeople with updates on industry changes and sales techniques in a variety of ways and will continue looking for more efficient ways of doing so.

- **Embracing Ethical Standards**—The mortgage industry meltdown was a notable indicator of a lapse in overall professionalism. Self-policing and government agency monitoring will ensure that salespeople in mortgage lending and most other fields will be held to higher standards than in the past. As evident with the mortgage industry, there will be a greater focus on licensing and registration so that consumers can monitor a salesperson's reputation. Salespeople will begin promoting their professional designations to an even greater degree, thereby distinguishing themselves from those who are not as "qualified."

  Salespeople will be extra vigilant in how they consult with and recommend programs and services to their clients. They will be especially concerned that a particular product really is best for the client, rather than an expedient solution to complete a quick sale and/or to boost the salesperson's income.

- **Keeping it Personal**—There will still be a need for salespeople to make a connection with customers, to match a face with the voice. The Internet has minimized the amount of "face time" required to excel in sales, but it has not eliminated the importance of maintaining personal relationships. I have purchased several cars without actually visiting the dealership, after viewing their "online showroom" and subsequently arranging the vehicle's delivery to my home. However, I had already developed a good rapport with the sales manager and was confident that it was the best possible deal.

  Salespeople will find it necessary to query customers and prospects on the way they wish to meet and stay in contact. It will most likely be a combination of in-person meetings, e-mail, online discussions on Skype and other venues.

PROFILE OF THE FUTURE SALESPERSON

The future salesperson will be better educated, knowledgeable, more professional and technology savvy than earlier salespeople. They will have better training in their specific industry and access to a greater array of resources.

- **Teams to Help Expand**—In some industries there will be more emphasis on team selling, the development of mutually beneficial alliances. Loan originators have done this successfully for years, with one or more "junior" salespeople supporting the lead loan officer's production. I believe that there will be more informal partnerships of salespeople working together as teams, for increased efficiencies and to ensure the customer's needs are met. For example, this might involve a financial planner, Realtor, CPA, loan originator and insurance advisor serving as the customer's financial services team.

  On the other hand, it is likely that fewer sales assistants will be needed, because greater online options will help streamline a company's operations. As more consumers apply for a mortgage or purchase a car on a website, there will be a reduction in the necessary administrative support. When an innovative company developed an online application program enabling borrowers to do most of the work in seeking a mortgage—selecting the loan based on established criteria, filling in required title information and completing the closing documentation—it set the stage for other industries to follow suit. There will be many such examples of less support staff being needed to help complete a sale.

- **Become a Specialist**—While there will still be room for the generalists—someone selling an entire product line—more industries will rely on specialists. With the increase in products and services, companies will want their salespeople to handle a specific product or two. I think it will become increasingly difficult to be a "jack of all trades." This should be more pronounced in service areas such as insurance and financial planning.

- **Welcoming an Enhanced Image**—Consumers will have a much higher regard for the sales profession. This will only occur as more standards are developed and as salespeople become more professional and better educated. The United Professional Sales Association has created a Professional Sales Ethics Framework, including an ethical Code of Conduct and a Buyer's Bill of Rights. In addition to following ethical practices, salespeople will contribute to the improved image by demonstrating their knowledge and customer-centric behavior. It takes time for multiple industries to adopt new guidelines and for salespeople to adhere to them on a regular basis, but the buying public will gradually notice the difference, especially as trade associations and individual companies promote their emphasis on professionalism in advertising, Website announcements, magazine articles and other forums. Consumers and others will have a greater respect for the salespeople they encounter in retail stores, offices and online outlets.

We will have to wait a while to see how much of my amateur forecasting is accurate. However, I am confident that our profession will be more rewarding on many fronts, and an even greater number of people will share my passion for sales.

Chapter Thirteen
A Formula for Thriving: The Gold Star Case History

"Experience taught me a few things. One is to listen to your gut, no matter how good something sounds on paper. The second is that you're generally better off sticking with what you know. And the third is that sometimes your best investments are the ones you don't make."

~Donald Trump

WHEN THE FIRST MAJOR hints of a mortgage industry crisis surfaced in mid-2007, I was determined that Gold Star Mortgage would not just survive.

We were not interested in surviving; we wanted to *thrive*, to excel while so many others were shutting their doors. There were hundreds of corporate failures during the infamous 2007-09 mortgage lending crisis. Some were quick fatalities, as company owners decided they could no longer endure the severe loss of business or were otherwise unable to compete. Others were slow, agonizing deaths of firms that struggled to hang on. I was determined that Gold Star would not be a casualty of this dark period.

I am convinced that many of the sales strategies highlighted in the preceding pages, combined with our overall operations strengths and the expertise of a strong management team, not only helped me maintain a high level of personal production, but also ensured that Gold Star would excel during an extremely difficult economic period. As I have emphasized to our employees, strategic partners and others, by applying the diverse strategies and related lessons, and then analyzing the results from Gold Star's inception through the lending industry crisis and beyond, we have developed an ideal case history that will be instructional for our company's future executive team members, as well as other management and sales leaders.

Surviving Versus Thriving

One of the unfortunate consequences of the lending crisis and resulting nationwide economic slump was a widespread emphasis on "surviving." I have heard so many salespeople at other companies say "I'm just trying to survive," which was seen as a major achievement. Of course, most people were not in the survival mode by choice; they were forced to do whatever was necessary to hold on to their companies and jobs. I am certainly not minimizing the challenges that lending industry professionals and others faced during this difficult time. My attitude was not due to an excess of hubris—believing that Gold Star would not be affected, that we were not vulnerable. However, our corporate culture has always been based on succeeding at a high level. Surviving means that you're in a holding pattern and not gaining market share. Thriving means your business and overall market share are increasing and you are poised for greater success in the near future. I simply refused to fall back into a failure mode that I had experienced at the beginning of my mortgage banking career. Of course, it would not be that simple.

The Subprime Swamp

An assortment of legislators, financial analysts and journalists has already dissected the subprime market and its contribution to the country's financial malaise. Those of us who actually work in the lending industry have our own unique perspective, one that may differ slightly from those who merely observed the prolonged "meltdown" from a safe distance. Who could have possibly imagined that there would be something actually called "liar loans?" These and other toxic loan products that were handed out during the 2003-07 subprime bonanza were a major reason that more than 300 lenders closed, many other businesses were shuttered, thousands of people lost their jobs, countless homeowners were forced into foreclosure, and the entire banking industry seemed to be on the brink of failing—all contributing significantly to the nation's most recent "great recession."

Actually, I and at least a few others sensed that something huge was going to happen. It wasn't that I was a seasoned forecaster, able to predict the industry's future. However, it did not take much more than common sense to notice the signs of this impending "perfect tsunami." *The Greatest Trade Ever* details John Paulson's bet against the mortgage industry, which netted his firm billions of dollars. As early as 2005, Paulson was predicting that the housing market would implode, dragging the economy down with it. I personally made a Paulson type bet as early as 2002. I refused to do subprime mortgages, regardless of how lucrative the commissions were. I knew that while allegedly helping many consumers purchase their homes, there were too many negative factors that could lead to massive problems.

I have always tried to stay one or two steps ahead of the market so I can gauge not only where the sales will be, but also the potential fallout of certain types of business and specific customer bases. For example, a few years back I could see clear evidence that the automotive Big Three were heading for serious financial trouble. The Michigan economy is highly dependent on the Big Three, and I realized that if they should go belly-up or encounter serious difficulty, much of my client base would disappear as well. Because of Michigan's precarious economic condition, I made the major decision to change the company from a primarily regional to a national focus. We began to expand our presence to states that were promising markets, such as Texas, Washington, Connecticut, Massachusetts and Oregon.

The hidden problems that were circulating throughout the American economy had yet to surface, but once they did it would result in nothing short of economic catastrophe. Of course, the biggest problem remained the subprime mortgage bubble. As the subprime machine revved up, new loan programs were regularly introduced that were increasingly risky to lenders and investors. In addition to the "basic" subprime loans there were "stated income loans" in which the bank did not undertake to verify the income of the borrowers to even see if they could afford the mortgage payments. These so-called "liar loans" would allow for a minimum wage borrower to obtain approval for a $500,000 home. I was amazed by one story of a California borrower who claimed an income of over $100,000 as a mariachi singer while financing a loan through a major lender. Since the borrower had no receipts or any way to prove that he did make $100,000+ as a mariachi singer, the decision makers determined it would be sufficient for him to take a picture in front of his house, dressed in a colorful mariachi costume. He did this and surprise, the loan was approved. Loans were approved for cashiers claiming excessive salaries at a certain mega-chain retailer and for car-washers who stated they had unbelievable assets. Indeed, a sufficient verification of employment during the subprime lending frenzy was to copy a Yellow Pages advertisement out of the phone book. Foreclosure proceedings can take years to complete, so technically a borrower could just decide to live in an oceanfront mansion for two or three years while the bank tried to evict them for non-payment. Frequently borrowers would move in to the house without the intention of ever making a payment, happy to have a place to live for a couple of years.

Early on, I realized the subprime market had grown out of control. Subprime loans had been in existence for years, but banks had been reluctant to enter into the market because of the risk of default. Any subprime loans that banks made were usually offset by mitigating factors such as extremely high borrower incomes or large amounts of liquid assets. When the mortgage-backed security concept became widely adopted, many financial institutions seemed to become especially greedy. Everyone wanted a piece of the subprime market, because the profit margins were so high and required relatively little work to achieve. When I was underwriting I had huge stacks of files dumped on my desk. Managers instructed us to verify that the address on the appraisal matched the loan application, and just look at the value on the appraisal. Then the file was to be cleared to close. Document deficiency was not a major concern. Eventually that digressed into loans where no appraisal was required, or where borrowers and loan officers seemed to be in collusion with appraisers to artificially inflate home values. Many companies put profitability and market share ahead of sound financial practices.

In 2000, subprime mortgages comprised slightly more than 5% of the market share; however by 2006 that number had grown to over 20%. It was estimated to encompass approximately 6.7 million loans valued at approximately $1.2 trillion. More than half had adjustable rate terms where the rate was constant for the first two to three years but then ballooned once the preliminary period was over. Almost 75% of the loans had prepayment penalties, meaning borrowers would have to pay extra money if they wanted to get out of their mortgage quicker. This ability to "reset" a subprime mortgage was a selling point at the outset. Borrowers were told that they could simply refinance their homes before their subprime loan adjusted upwards and this would allow them to take advantage of a fixed interest rate down the road. Setting aside the fact that fixed interest rates are tied to market indexes and there is no guarantee that they would prove to be more beneficial, the theory also failed from the presumption that home values would continue to appreciate. They didn't. When housing prices took a nosedive, subprime borrowers who were highly leveraged did not qualify for a refinance, and were left with a rate that adjusted dramatically upward.

There was a huge appetite for these exotic loans and our office phones rang incessantly as borrowers inquired about them. "Can I get one from you?" and "How long does it take to get approved?" they would ask. You could hear the excitement in their voices when they realized they could get a half-million-dollar house while simultaneously being under or unemployed. However, I explained to these disappointed prospects that I did not believe in these products and refused to sell them. In addition, subprime loans didn't fit into our business model. My longstanding goal was to create a network of loyal customers who would refer their friends, family members and work associates to me. I knew that most subprime borrowers generally were hesitant to discuss their loan with others and not inclined to make referrals. The opportunity to have my customer base increase exponentially would substantially diminish if I climbed aboard the "subprime train."

During this period, many people seemed to be leaving their professions in order to become a loan originator, with the prospect of earning thousands of dollars a day. What is more disturbing, however, was the fact that there was hardly any institutional control on subprime lending. In many states, loan originators weren't required to have a license, meaning people with little or no financial experience, no educational background and even questionable criminal history records were considered to have the capabilities to advise homeowners on their financial affairs. Most of these individuals did not even know how a mortgage worked, which was especially troublesome to me given the amount of time that I had spent trying to learn the business.

New subprime lending shops were entering the market at a rapid pace, and were often caught up in the luxurious lifestyle. I was amazed by the story of a Seattle, Washington-based company that hired loan officers straight out of high school and put them through a short training program. They took 30 minutes to describe how a loan was processed, a skill that I spent almost a decade mastering. After a few other quick courses, they were considered ready to advise homeowners on their financial well-being. The office itself came complete with a gym, indoor waterfall, and extravagant murals, all for a reported $13 million price tag. There were also stories of other excessive behavior, including wild parties.

I later read a Forbes Magazine article that profiled a former mortgage broker who served three years in prison in the early 2000's for mortgage fraud. While in prison, he spent his time teaching the mortgage business to other inmates who strived for a better life. The author referred to the mortgage business as a more lucrative and safer business then the drug trade and how it became the most sought after profession for prisoners. There was a waiting list for the class, which I thought was quite ironic. The subprime market was a train wreck waiting to happen...in 2007.

The Shoes Kept Dropping

While I was previously aware of the likely trouble ahead, the alarm bell sounded loudly when the first lenders began announcing their demise in July 2007. First it was the subprime specialists who began to crumble. Then other lenders, banks and affiliated companies got caught in the vortex. It was clear that even the most successful lenders and others associated with the mortgage lending industry were not immune to the mounting difficulties. Every day there was another major announcement about a lender closing or a Wall Street company in trouble. Mortgageimplode.com, the site that listed corporate casualties, became the most popular place to obtain industry information. It quickly made the "Favorites List" on my employees' Web browsers. Morning water cooler chat often included a game of "guess which company is next." Size had nothing to do with it. The largest and smallest of banks were all suffering the losses. There were numerous stories of CEOs or other top managers hastily calling their people together or making a conference call to announce their company's imminent closure.

One of the most startling developments occurred one day in our corporate offices. On October 25, 2007, we were meeting with our Bank of America Account Executive in a Gold Star conference room. He reassured us that his employer was committed to the mortgage business. While he was talking, I received a call from his regional manager who said "I understand you're all in the Gold Star conference room. Would you please leave the room for a minute?" I stepped outside and asked, "What's going on?" There was a brief silence and then his bewildered answer: "I can't believe they just shut us down." When I returned to the conference room I tried to remain calm, not wanting to reveal to the account executive that he and hundreds of his coworkers had just lost their jobs. Bank of America's Wholesale Division became casualty #169 on the Mortgage Implode list and would no longer be a source of funds for thousands of mortgage brokers. The general response was "If it can happen to B of A, everybody better watch out."

Obviously, the financial meltdown required a major shift in my overall focus. More than ever, I felt the responsibility of over 1,500 people (employees and families) leaning on me. I was enjoying a very successful career, but the company's future was not about me. My overriding goal was preserving the jobs and the livelihood of Gold Star employees. I recall sitting at my desk one early morning and thinking about the options. In the most extreme situation, I knew I could always close the office and resume originating from a small suite or a home office and do extremely well. However, that was a fleeting thought, as I wanted to continue developing what we had started. We had several excellent managers who were making major contributions to the company's success, but somehow I felt that it was primarily up to me to guide us through the lending industry's quagmire.

In fact, I may have taken this responsibility to the extreme. In January 2008 I took a weekend skiing trip to Aspen, Colorado, which given my difficulty taking non-working vacations in even the best of circumstances, may not have been the wisest decision. I remember my first ski run, heading down the mountain on a picture perfect afternoon. As I passed a group of skiers, I suddenly thought of everyone back at our corporate headquarters and other Gold Star offices. What if I fell and broke my leg? Even though I knew I wasn't irreplaceable, this was absolutely not the time to be on the injured reserve list. I skied safely down the hill, went straight to the lodge and called Rick to see how everyone was doing. It was my only ski run and my last vacation for two years.

There Was No Manual

There was no manual for dealing with the ongoing crisis. We were not able to refer to a book or contingency plan that offered the answers. We had to assess the damage and create a road map for the next three, six, nine months and so on. I was now devoting more time to general management than ever before, and I resumed the demanding work schedule I had when we first started Gold Star.

It was critical that we maintain constant communications with our staff. My open door policy was especially timely, as nervous employees were often lined up waiting to be assured that we were going to weather this tsunami. We began holding twice-weekly teleconferences to provide updates and several times a day I e-mailed new industry developments, policy changes and other announcements to our staff. The ongoing communications helped to keep everyone going in the same direction, making sure that we remained a team on a shared mission. My public speaking ability was definitely tested on several occasions, including September 8,

2008 when it was announced that Fannie Mae and Freddie Mac could be heading for receivership and I explained the news to our staff. A week later, I had to review an even more startling development: Lehman Brothers crashing. On September 15, I invited everyone in to the conference room so that I could explain what had happened. There were many somber faces as I provided the basic details surrounding Lehman's bankruptcy, following the rumors of its failed assets. There were also many urgent questions: *What does this mean to us?*, *Is this industry really a house of cards?*, and *When is it going to stop?*, were a few of the milder ones. Of course, I did not have all the answers; no one did. I did not try to minimize the negative news, but rather to emphasize the relatively strong position Gold Star was in. "No one knows just how long this will last, but it will certainly continue for the next year or so," I said. "However, we are in a better position than the companies that have failed so far, and many of the others that are still in business. First, we are not burdened by a subprime portfolio," I stressed. "We have initiated strict guidelines to further protect ourselves from any significant losses. We also have more than adequate reserves and I am willing to invest my personal funds as necessary." I also talked about the opportunity to expand the business. I answered their questions, but knew that we all shared common concerns.

We had similar impromptu meetings to discuss the subsequent developments of the imploding banking lending industry, such as the rumors that the government was planning to nationalize all of the country's banks. We had to motivate and reassure people that not only would they continue to have a place to work, but that we had a unique opportunity to generate revenue and to establish ourselves as a business leader.

It was equally important to maintain close contact with our lenders and customers. I had daily phone conversations with top managers at our major banks and lenders. We shared our own insights as to what was occurring and what we were doing to maintain our company positions. Certainly at times it was difficult to know whether or not everyone was providing the most detailed responses, but we had to accept a level of mutual trust, difficult as that might be

---

NO RECESSION HERE

DATE: September 15, 2008

TO: Gold Star Employees

FROM: Dan Milstein

RE: Don't Think About a Recession

It's no secret that the mortgage lending industry—and the general economy—isn't in the best shape right now. We have discussed this in company meetings and various other communications. We have witnessed the failure of many companies and seen an avalanche of bad news.

However, as I have repeatedly stressed—we are not going to participate in any anticipated recession. We will continue doing what has made this company successful—providing our customers with the best possible loan product and available rates, along with stellar service.

With interest rates coming down, this is a great time for your customers and prospects to refinance. Work your database, make calls to everyone you know.

Together we will continue succeeding in this difficult period.

---

at times. Of course we were also an information source for customers who were concerned about their current loan and future mortgages. Some customers had been in the midst of a loan transaction that was now in jeopardy and were anxious that they would not be able to recover. They also were concerned about the never-ending series of articles and TV broadcasts about the lending industry's missteps and how mortgage brokers and lenders were responsible for the current economic nightmare facing the country. Many people did not take the time to understand how complex the situation really was and the pivotal role that Wall Street played.

Throughout this period, I and other Gold Star managers made a point to stay as upbeat as possible. One of our constant phrases was, "Gold Star will not participate in a recession." We were obviously aware of the gravity of the lending industry's and the nation's fragile economic condition. However, we wanted to maintain a positive outlook and make all employees confident that our company would endure. That does not mean that I wasn't worried about the industry's and Gold Star's future. I had many sleepless nights, especially during the first six months of the meltdown.

Capitalizing on the New Market

I certainly was sympathetic about the problems so many companies were facing. At the same time, while numerous lenders were falling out of business, we saw an opportunity to expand. Over 50 percent of our competition was gone within two years and the talent pool was getting increasingly full. Loan originators who had received multi-million dollar bonuses from previous employers and would not have considered working at Gold Star were now asking us about job openings. Suddenly, we were an attractive option. Gold Star moved to a massive expansion mode. Rather than launch our own new offices in various cities, we thought the best approach would be to add loan originators who could bring their portfolio of loyal customers, which in a few cases meant taking over offices that major firms had closed. We also got daily calls from senior managers and support staff who were anxious to find a permanent position.

In addition, we increased our marketing program, when others were drastically reducing theirs. Our advertising message was simple: stability and growth. We reassured customers and the general public that we had many options for the loans and despite the bad news they heard on an almost daily basis, Gold Star was doing well and would continue to thrive.

With a clean balance sheet and viable lender relationships, we were one of the few growing companies that could operate effectively and efficiently. Our non-bureaucratic mentality allowed us to adapt quickly to the volatile market, making necessary changes "on the fly." In 2008, we opened four new offices and increased our workforce by 25 percent, as so many other firms were dismissing people and closing their doors. We would double that expansion in 2009.

Wise Counsel

During much of this tumultuous period, I was able to complement my own experience and judgment with the counsel of others I respected. For example, in addition to consulting with our managers on a daily basis, I frequently talked to my close friend, Matt Roslin, the chief legal officer at one of our major banks. He had a great understanding of the nuances of the lending industry's challenges and how companies could remain solvent and viable by withstanding the legal, political and other pressures. His expertise regarding potential regulatory reform was especially valuable.

TEN KEYS TO SURVIVING DIFFICULT TIMES

1. *Preserve capital.*

2. *Maintain maximum liquidity.*

3. *If not profitable cut expenses down to where you break even.*

4. *Be prepared to fire friends.*

5. *Credit quality matters more than ever.*

6. *Stop paying outrageous commissions or salaries.*

7. *Commit to better financial reporting: If you can't measure it, you can't manage it.*

8. *Only hire people from companies that have been successful.*

9. *Have a written plan. Figure out what you need to be profitable, and stick to the plan.*

10. *Focus only on the things you can control*

I also benefited from many lengthy discussions I had with Joe Garrett, a consultant whom a bank asked to perform an audit of our financial health. In late 2008, I met Joe, a partner of Garrett and Watts, and a savvy veteran of the lending industry. We developed a good rapport and I was fortunate to receive his input on a number of topics. Among other advice, he shared his keys to surviving difficult times, which in some ways was a refresher course in crisis management. I really took his advice to heart, especially point #8 about hiring people who had been very successful at other companies and who brought no unwanted baggage with them. I was careful to do an extensive review of all new loan originator candidates. This was a valid point, because the industry had certainly attracted a large number of unethical and otherwise undesirable people.

When the global financial meltdown hit, I was confident we would thrive, even though I faced many difficult days and sleepless nights. By the end of 2008, we had close to 220 employees. Gold Star didn't lay off any employees and no one quit because of the difficult environment. The company had grown 200 percent and achieved a 712 percent increase in our total revenue during the most difficult time imaginable.

Promising Signs

At the beginning of 2010, the picture looked brighter, but we, and everyone else in the industry, still faced a difficult period. Of course, I was particularly gratified that the bold moves I made in the previous few years had paid off. For example, I was acutely aware that my decision to avoid the subprime market during 2004-07 could have turned out to be a major blunder. While it was not part of our business model and I fervently believed that these loans would eventually prove disastrous, I could have been wrong. If the market hadn't blown up, the subprime lenders might have been the ones holding the bag of gold and Gold Star could well have been a minor player in the lending industry. Our revenue could have stalled and we probably would not have been able to grow at the level we did, nor have the opportunity to hire some of the industry's top talent. Some of our loan originators would have become disenchanted with my decision-making capability and likely departed for other companies. Certainly I had made other potential risky decisions, but avoiding the subprime arena was at the top of the list. However, it was the right move and we passed through the storm largely unscathed.

Another positive note was that we were seeing fewer tier one lenders shutting down at this time, since the market was somewhat calmer. Meanwhile, competition continued to decrease and we had the infrastructure in place to handle a major influx of new business. Gold Star also was generating significant volume in government lending, which we previously had not actively pursued. In late 2009 we realized an unanticipated boost in government loan production and determined that this would continue to be a viable base for the future.

National Footprint

During 2007-09 we developed a model for office expansion, which we continued in 2010-2011. Our goal remained the same: to find struggling but potentially strong mortgage companies needing the infrastructure that Gold Star could offer. Rather than build offices from the ground up, we prefer to identify successful originators who formerly worked for companies that either closed or were otherwise looking for a new opportunity, and who had developed a loyal following in their communities.

There isn't an ironclad formula to finding the right people; it involves a series of meetings, careful analysis of their past performance, and a little luck. When we think there is a good fit "on paper," we meet and listen carefully to their goals. It is essential that new salespeople don't feel they are maxed out on their sales potential, that they still have the drive to increase their production. We want people who believe there is no ceiling to what they can accomplish. We typically discount their first year projections by 30 percent, because experience has shown that a new office never gets started as planned. Although it is important that all our salespeople share the common attributes of being high volume producers and a "there is no limit to what I can accomplish" mentality, we certainly don't require that they all possess the same backgrounds. Our loan originators include a former attorney, doctor, clothing company executive and professional golfer. Their distinct experiences have helped enhance their sales and customer service skills.

From a geographic standpoint, we are interested in increasing our presence in what we refer to as the "fortunate" states, those that have more favorable economic climates, and have avoided double digit unemployment, significant housing slumps and other negative growth indicators. In 2010 and 2011 we added offices in California, Colorado and Texas. We also developed new branches in Michigan and Florida, when highly experienced originators from key markets became available after their previous companies closed.

At the same time, our cross-selling opportunities were flourishing. During the previous three years, we had introduced financial planning, insurance and credit repair divisions. While mortgage lending continues to be 90 percent of our total business, we knew diversification into these other areas would benefit customers and increase Gold Star's bottom line. We did have to overcome the hesitancy of some salespeople who initially found cross selling these programs somewhat more difficult than their colleagues. They had been accustomed to a single task: providing mortgages. Now they not only had to accept the value of offering the additional services, but also had to be sufficiently knowledgeable to answer questions and close deals.

Management Transition

For some time I knew a major change would be necessary to ensure our long-term growth. We were now one of the largest lenders in the Midwest with a growing national presence; it was no longer "Dan's company." We had to consider the potential of hiring a chief operating officer who was experienced at guiding a company to the next level, with an emphasis on operations and finance. This was obviously a big step. However, it was clear that adding a well respected industry veteran would enhance our credibility with the larger banks with whom we wanted to do business on a regular basis. I had gradually realized there is a distinct prejudice towards CEOs who are also their company's founder. The belief is that often they are not able to look at the company objectively; that they are too close to clearly see the organization's faults and make hard decisions to rectify them. This seems to be a gross generalization and I didn't necessarily include myself in that category but also understood that if this was the prevailing attitude, we should adapt accordingly.

Some of my associates and others thought I would find it extremely difficult to relinquish any company control and hire a COO. Perhaps they reasoned that after devoting almost 10 years to running the company, my ego would not allow a newcomer to have a free rein in the necessary decision-making. However, it was actually an easy choice; I knew that a COO could further enhance our operational and financial disciplines, while I could concentrate on sales and long-term planning.

Of course, deciding on a COO is not easy for any organization. The key is to find the person who has the ideal blend of experience, commitment to excellence, and a belief in your culture. In the past, we had senior manager candidates who had overtly promoted their own agenda, with little regard to what makes Gold Star unique, and we didn't want to risk a similar situation with a new operations chief. I was not looking for a clone, someone who possessed a duplicate of my background and skills, but rather an innovative and savvy business leader who could add an extra dimension to what we already had. I met with our top managers and explained the goals and process by which we would select someone. The basic requirements included:

- Familiar and experienced in sales, the foundation of Gold Star's success.

- Well-rounded in business. We didn't want someone whose main success story was the subprime niche.

- Experience in helping a company rise to the next level.

- An appreciation of our focus on customer service.

- Comfortable with our goals/culture, not trying to shepherd their own agenda.

- Energetic and enthusiastic, not someone who was worn out and looking for a "last stop before retiring."

After contacting a few well-connected sources, we soon had more than 200 résumés, primarily from highly experienced business professionals, many of whom had been displaced by the lending crisis. David Prichard was one of those frequently mentioned, although I did not think he was available. I knew he had a great reputation and background, including his senior management positions at AmTrust and InterFirst. I thought his background as a CPA would be a definite plus, ensuring he had the expertise to oversee the company's financial health. We also shared a common tie; before starting Golden Rule, I was one of 800 people who reported to him at InterFirst, although I was certain that he was not aware of my presence then.

AN OBJECTIVE VIEW

I knew that Gold Star was quite successful and the COO opening seemed intriguing, but I didn't know what to expect from my meeting with Dan. After a few minutes of introductions and small talk he got right to the point. He explained that Gold Star was growing quickly and doing well financially, that there were challenges ahead and he needed an experienced person to help expand operations, quality control, compliance and other areas. We shared the same philosophy of hard work and providing a family atmosphere. From the beginning I knew Gold Star was a good business model. My goal wasn't to rock the boat, but rather to have everyone understand that I'm here to support them. At the same time, Dan made a point to emphasize: "Don't tell me how beautiful I am – I don't want a yes man." He was looking for helpful, honest feedback. Egos are definitely checked at the door here. This is an inspiring place to be and I'm glad to have the chance to have a measurable impact."

—David Prichard, Gold Star COO

I narrowed the list of candidates to Dave and two other top finalists. My half-hour meeting with Dave turned into a four-hour, free-ranging discussion during which we covered a wide variety of topics. I was impressed with his experience taking companies through increasing levels of growth. He also came from an organization that valued a family environment, which was definitely a critical factor. I had the sense that he would not be intent in making wholesale changes just to show he was in control. He said he respected what we had already accomplished and desired to help us build on that. I shared the unabridged version of our company history and my view of the future, and opened the books for his review. At the end of our lengthy mutual interview, we shook hands and I told Dave we would make a quick decision. After some additional discussion with our senior managers, I called Dave the next day to offer him the COO position. It was one of the best decisions I have made.

On his first day with Gold Star, we welcomed Dave with a large stack of files to digest. He and I began meeting several times a day to formulate weekly and monthly plans. He was known as a tireless worker, and salespeople and staff found him to be very approachable. Although he didn't make rash decisions or sweeping changes during his first days on the job, his presence was definitely felt. Within a few weeks he had reorganized Gold Star's back office systems, which greatly streamlined our processes.

Dave also realized how much we value a sense of humor. He had only been here a few days when he received another Gold Star welcome. We had a plumber install a new toilet in one of the bathrooms and he threw the old one away. I thought of a much better use. When Dave walked into his office one early morning, he saw the toilet where his office chair had been, along with a bottle of premium champagne. I think he laughed the loudest while several people took pictures.

We continued to strengthen the management team by adding a chief financial officer, compliance manager and a mergers and acquisitions manager. Expanding our senior management group "brain trust" did not alter our ability to make decisions and implement plans expeditiously. When we were much smaller, I developed a simple form that we could use to decide on key capital expenditures, such as a phone or computer system, and other critical plans. I asked anyone proposing a new project or program to outline the pros and cons so that we could quickly consider and make a decision. We have always applied the same basic principal to any substantial proposal, whether it be a new office, policy change or management hire. This enables us to do a thorough, but relatively brief analysis and make the appropriate decision. We do not suffer from analysis paralysis. This is a big problem for many organizations started by entrepreneurs who later add too many layers of management and bureaucratic policies, and become unable to move fast enough to capitalize on important opportunities.

As we continued through the industry's post-meltdown phase, Gold Star embarked on another major step—creating a succession plan, something that I definitely hadn't anticipated when I started the company. More than ever, I realized how important it was to safeguard the interests of Gold Star and its employees. In addition to any unforeseen accident or other emergency that could hinder my responsibilities, I knew that eventually I would assume a lesser role. Unlike some business CEOs who select someone to succeed them but then decide to "un-retire," at some point in the future I would indeed leave the day-to-day management to others and possibly pursue other interests. Creating a succession plan is not an easy assignment. It forces you to step back and examine your personal ambitions, company directives and most important, the ideal replacement candidates. Even though there would be no immediate changes, I realized that this was the beginning of what would be a major change to the company and my personal life. However, I knew that when the time was right, I would gladly move aside and let someone else take the captain's chair to help make Gold Star even more successful.

Welcome Recognition

Recognition has never been one of my overriding goals, yet it was good to see that other lenders, business leaders and customers were noticing us. During the last few years, Gold Star has been recognized on a regional and national level. In 2009 and 2010, *Inc. Magazine* ranked us as one of the fastest growing U.S. companies and during the same period we also were rated as one of the Top Work Places in Michigan by the Detroit Free Press. One of my most satisfying moments was reading the Free Press one Sunday morning and seeing that we had been voted a top work place by our employees. Reading the testimonials they had written was one of the first times since leaving Kiev that I actually shed a few tears. We were also pleased when Gold Star was selected as one of "Michigan's Economic Bright Spots" in 2011.

I was also included in the "40 Under 40" list by National Mortgage Professional magazine, as one of the 40 most influential mortgage professionals under the age of 40, and a similar "Top 40 Executives" published in Crain's Detroit Business.

True Value

Reaching our 10-year anniversary in October 2010 was a tremendous milestone. On October 18, the actual day we began doing business as Gold Star a decade earlier, we had a full-page ad in the Detroit News and Free Press, thanking our employees and business partners for helping to make this milestone a reality. That morning I sat in my office and thought of what was most important to Gold Star. It was an easy answer—the employees who worked long hours to help make Gold Star a success and the family members who were supportive of their commitment. I was certainly proud that we had achieved recognition and financial success, but more than anything I was happy about the group of people who worked at our headquarters and other offices throughout the country, including several who had previously been among our biggest competitors and most vocal critics. I personally delivered a copy of the newspaper to all of our headquarters employees and told them how much I appreciated their service. We also had it delivered to all of our other offices and I received many congratulatory calls that day. This was an extremely satisfying occasion.

Future Forward

In the last several years, Gold Star has grown from a successful company working with a predominantly Michigan base to 400 employees in 25 offices located throughout the country. The company has an unlimited future, and is on a fast track to assume its place as a

MONDAY, OCT. 18, 2010   WWW.FREEP.COM   **5A**

Gold Star
Mortgage Financial Group

Letter from the President

October 18, 2010

Dear Friends,

Today is a special occasion for Gold Star Mortgage Financial Group – our 10th anniversary. We could not have achieved this significant milestone without you – our dedicated employees, supportive business partners and many loyal customers.

Since assisting our first customers in October 2000, Gold Star has grown from a modest, 300-square foot office with two people to more than 400 employees now based in our Southeast Michigan headquarters, as well as 20 branch offices in five states. Looking back on our humble beginnings, I am proud that our company remains committed to the family values that form the foundation of Gold Star.

Our mortgage business has evolved dramatically through an era of radical change in the financial industry. We attribute much of the company's ability to adapt to our staff's knowledge, experience and flexibility. I am fortunate to be associated with such an amazing group of individuals, who strive daily to make a positive impact on the people and communities we serve in Michigan and across the country. These people are passionate about providing clients with a high level of personalized service. I am grateful and humbled by their contributions to Gold Star's development—as a business and a family.

I am also proud that we have been ranked for two consecutive years as the Top Workplace by the Detroit Free Press, and as one of the fastest growing companies in America by Inc. Magazine. This would not have been possible without the support of everyone at Gold Star.

While we have experienced numerous changes during the last decade, our primary focus has remained the same: to provide our clients with access to the best rates and a variety of mortgage products. Gold Star's high standards help ensure our customers receive mortgage-based savings and increased knowledge to properly manage and control their financial well-being. We are grateful for the key role that they continue to play in our success.

It is with the utmost gratitude that I ask you to join me in saying something that should make us all proud: Happy 10th Birthday Gold Star, with many more to come!

Very Truly Yours,

Daniel Milstein
Chief Executive Officer
Gold Star Mortgage Financial Group
(800) 201-LOAN (5626)

EQUAL HOUSING
OPPORTUNITY

major lender and a business leader on a national scale. Certainly there are challenges ahead. The lending industry is more regulated than ever, the general economic environment threatens all business sectors, and customers have become more questioning. Gold Star will continue to focus on market share, profitability and employee training to make sure everyone is prepared for the new marketplace.

I have had many people—including some of our top managers, family members and friends ask "So, what's next for you?" Of course, the logical conclusion would be that I have a master plan that details my every step for the next five to 10 years. Actually that is not the case. My main focus is simple—guaranteeing Gold Star's success. I intend to keep selling, helping the company grow and working with new people to help them reach their own objectives. Along the way, I know we will have some fun, whether it is with our incentive contests, staff get-togethers or late night brainstorming sessions.

When I first enjoyed success as a loan originator after my two earlier failures, I set several goals to achieve before reaching 40. I wanted to start and run a successful company, regularly appear on the nationwide "Top Originator List," be financially secure and write a book. I have met those and several additional goals, but as most people do, I find there are always new heights to aspire to. It has been a rewarding professional and personal journey so far. I am confident that the best years are ahead. I look forward to seeing what happens next.

Epilogue
My American Dream

"You give before you get."
~Napoleon Hill

As a young boy in Kiev, I don't recall specifically thinking of "the American Dream." My version of it has changed dramatically since I first came here as a nervous teenager. When we arrived in this country in 1991, our family's immediate goal was to simply get settled, acclimated to a country with which we were not familiar. Then our focus became finding jobs so that we would not have to depend on donated clothes and food stamps. Of course, I wanted to make a few friends, learn to speak English and graduate from high school. Once I saw the possibilities, I expanded my horizon; I planned to graduate from college and then develop a career path, earn a reasonable income, have a family and hopefully buy a home.

Even when I encountered the inevitable obstacles and failed at a specific challenge, I never felt that success, whatever that meant at the time, was out of reach. I always had faith that if I continued to work hard, be a good citizen and never give up, I would eventually realize most of my goals, however modest they might be. That didn't necessarily mean I would be a top salesman, nationally recognized in my profession or run my own company. Growing up I simply wanted to have a satisfying career, whether that turned out to be working as a McDonald's manager, as a teacher or as a businessman. I truly believe that I would have been content with almost any profession, as long as it was in this country.

❈ ❈ ❈

As a teenager, I wondered if Americans took their advantages for granted. I thought that because they had never lived in a more oppressive or otherwise unfriendly country, they couldn't appreciate the great opportunities awaiting them, the way immigrants did. They grow up expecting the promise of a bright future, the amazing benefit of American-born citizenship. I had become friends with two Russian boys whose families came to the United States a few years before mine, and we often talked about the difference between us and our other classmates. It wasn't that we felt sorry for ourselves, having to leave our home to get a "second chance" at what everyone else knew was their birthright. Rather, it was as if we had our own secret from the others; that we alone understood that this was truly "the land of opportunity."

In our high school history class we read about the immigrants who came to this country and overcame various obstacles to become extremely successful, including Albert Einstein, Irving Berlin and Joseph Pulitzer. My own parents embodied the spirit of the American Dream. Even as we were living in our first cramped apartment, they promised each other they would own a house sooner rather than later. My father, a former engineer, worked the night shift at a plastics factory, and my mother, an economist in Kiev, went back to school so she could find a job as a medical assistant. Within three years, they had saved enough money to buy a home, and I was able to help by contributing some of my McDonald's earnings.

Another role model was my Uncle Igor Keselman who fled to America in 1980, and after extensive retraining, got a good job as an engineer at one of the Chrysler plants. His son Gene was five years old when they emigrated, and is now a Major in the United States Air Force. They proved that it was perfectly acceptable to dream big. As role models, I could relate more to their stories than those of Einstein and other celebrity immigrants.

I got my own close-up look at an earlier generation of immigrants when I joined my two Russian friends on a road trip to

New York. While there, we visited Ellis Island, the gateway to a new life for so many people. In the museum we stared intently at the old photos of families shown as they left the ships that had brought them from Ireland, Italy, and elsewhere. I tried to imagine what it must have been like for these scared, tired and hopeful foreigners, arriving with just a suitcase of clothes and a few other belongings. Of course, it was easy for me to relate to. Instead of traveling on a crowded ship and getting a glimpse of the Statue of Liberty as the first sign of freedom, our lengthy journey ended after a long wait in custom lines and a final stop at the Detroit Airport.

Lifelong Dreams

During the last decade, I have gained an even deeper appreciation of what the American dream really means. I realized early on that it doesn't guarantee success or happiness, only the possibility of succeeding. Immigrants are given a blank canvas and it is up to us to create a meaningful life, to never stop striving to improve ourselves. After the initial obstacles I faced, it would have been easy to lower the bar on my goals, to accept something less. For me, that would have been neglecting the sacrifices that my parents made to help secure the opportunity. Each time I faced a new challenge, I reminded myself why we came here, and the importance of persevering.

I have also enjoyed watching my younger brother Alex embracing the challenges of starting a new life in America. While I may have thought it was easier for him because children are usually more adaptable to new surroundings, he still faced the same basic difficulties I did. He was just eight years old when he started school in Michigan. I like to think that he learned from some of my "trial and error" mistakes. He did become conversant in the English language faster than the rest of us, and was definitely on a faster track to success. When he was only 14 years old, Alex got a job answering phones for a real estate company. Two years later, two agents hired him to develop their Website. He obtained his community college Associates degree the day before he graduated from high school at 17, received his real estate license the following year, and graduated from college when he was only 19. Alex has since become one of our county's top two real estate agents and a well-regarded community member. His is a true success story.

❈ ❈ ❈

I had another affirmation of the significance of the American Dream when I returned to the former USSR in 2007, the first time since our departure in 1991. A professional hockey player friend was traveling to Moscow and invited me to accompany him, suggesting that I could make a stopover in Kiev. I had reservations about going back because I didn't have pleasant memories, and there was not much I really cared to see. However, I finally decided it would be worthwhile to make the trip for some type of closure, a final reminder that our decision to leave was the right one. Perhaps I would even meet up with a few of my boyhood friends.

As I arrived in Kiev, I noticed two obvious signs that it was quite different from what I remembered. First, the streets were more congested with auto traffic. Second, there were modern stores that actually had enough food on their shelves. In other ways Kiev seemed just the same, especially the worn-looking apartment buildings. I called two of my old friends and we arranged to meet and drive around the city, stopping at the places that were such a big part of our early lives. We saw our school, neighborhood churches, the black market area that is now a popular farmers' bazaar, and even my old apartment.

During our brief tour, we talked about growing up, playing ice hockey and soccer in the streets, and our current lives. I was hesitant to discuss my current banking profession in much detail. Certainly I was proud of what I had accomplished in my adopted country, but I felt that somehow it would put an even greater distance between us. I knew that if I had stayed there, I probably would be working in the same factory that many friends did. We were from different worlds now. Where once we were the closest of friends, at this point it seemed we were mere acquaintances, separated not only by 6,200 miles, but also divergent cultures, life experiences and future ambitions. It was almost as if I had never lived there. That trip made me appreciate America even more. How different life would have been if we had remained in Ukraine.

❈ ❈ ❈

Whenever possible, I try to share my own American dream story so that others understand how grateful the majority of immigrants are. Most important, I have made sure that my young daughter is aware of and appreciates her heritage. We have talked about what it was like to live in Russia, the Chernobyl catastrophe and why her grandparents chose to leave. I also explain that her fortunate lifestyle is not necessarily the norm, that she needs to study, go to college and become a productive member of society. I believe she is proud of being a second generation Russian and an American born citizen. I also include the "follow your dream" theme when I speak to university classes, business groups and even informal gatherings of our employees. I like to tell people that "I came here with nothing and America gave me everything."

Part of the message I share is that while I possess complete freedom of expression now—to write a letter to the editor complaining about presidential policies or contest a traffic ticket, I choose not to voice any dissent. I tell people that the worst day in America, because of any real or perceived problems, is preferable over the best day in so many other countries, including my former homeland.

While not everyone can identify with my journey to and life in America, I feel that the essence of my "immigrant to CEO" story resonates with most people.

Giving Back

Obviously, I have not reached my American dream alone. My parents had the foresight and courage to get us to this country. There were a couple of high school teachers who had the patience to help me become more conversant in the English language. McDonald's gave an inexperienced but ambitious teenager a chance to prove himself. I was fortunate to get a fresh start at InterFirst. Of course, the Owens' offered the key to the biggest door I wanted to open, starting my first real business. Many others at Gold Star and elsewhere have been instrumental in helping me achieve personal and professional goals. I realize that many immigrants have not been as fortunate as I was navigating through the maze of American life. They have not received the same guidance and encouragement and haven't been able to realize their full potential.

I believe that anyone who has the American dream should give something back. While it is likely that many immigrants are more concerned with receiving the benefits and even taking advantage of "the system," I am hopeful that most also make the effort to contribute. As a high school student, I remember reading about President John Kennedy's famous speech, when he said "Ask not what your country can do for you, ask what you can do for your country." I realized even then that the country had already done a great deal for my family, just helping us get started. I was not sure how to give back, but was certain that one day I would have that chance.

My first experience involved helping other Russian immigrants get established, find an apartment or purchase a car. Later, I was grateful that Gold Star was able to give many people jobs. In addition, I like to support worthwhile organizations that benefit the community. For example, when a local community center that aids lower income families lost its funding, I offered to cover half of their budget for the year and 10 percent of its total budget for another five years. I have been fortunate to be able to donate money to various other organizations and individuals. I am especially excited about a new scholarship fund that I am developing, which will help other low income students achieve their dream of attending college. Giving back does not have to be on a grand scale; it doesn't require large donations or working extra jobs. There are numerous ways to accomplish this, such as mentoring others in need or volunteering at a social services agency.

✖ ✖ ✖

Today, I don't think of pursuing the "dream" the same way that I did when we first landed on American soil. I am still as excited to be an American as the day we came here, and later when I was sworn in as a citizen. I don't take my past achievements for granted and always look forward to new possibilities. Having realized a certain level of success, I am no longer as concerned about meeting a series of goals to validate the golden opportunity this country has afforded me. Yet, there are frequent reminders that make me stop and reflect on how far I have come. For example, seeing my daughter playing with her friends in our large backyard, away from a crowded city street; listening to a group of people in a coffee shop have a spirited debate about national politics, without fear of being overheard; walking through the door of our company headquarters to see employees working hard to make their own dreams come true. At those inspirational moments I think, *Can you imagine arriving here as a 16 year-old kid with only 17 cents in your pocket, unable to speak English with no clue about what the future would be, and to be where you are now?* I smile and remind myself, *Only in America.*

Appendix

Accolades and Accomplishments

"It is important that you recognize your progress and take pride in your accomplishments. Share your achievements with others. Brag a little. The recognition and support of those around you is nurturing."

~Rosemarie Rossetti

NUMBERS CAN CERTAINLY SPEAK for themselves. At Gold Star we certainly have plenty of numbers that by themselves tell a compelling story. But numbers alone don't convey the hidden truths that lie behind them. Any business can occasionally get lucky, but no business succeeds on a sustained basis without the drive, determination, and ingenuity of its people.

Give a person a job they hate doing and they'll drag their feet, reach for all kinds of excuses and struggle to complete it. When they do, it's often of less than acceptable quality. Give them something they love to do, and they become unstoppable. The urge to overachieve—and be recognized—shines through. All manner of creative ingenuity and dedication of time will go into getting the best possible job completed on or ahead of time. It's in our nature. On the pages that follow, hopefully, these claims come to life in the very nature of Gold Star Mortgage Financial Group. Not only have we consistently outperformed competitors in such measures as loan volume, but we've done it while being among the most desirable places to work.

LETTER TO EMPLOYEES ON GOLD STAR'S REPEAT WIN OF TOP WORKPLACE ACCOLADE

Dear Friends,

I am happy to announce that Gold Star has once again been named a Top Workplace in Michigan. This marks the second straight year that we have achieved such an honor, and I am pleased to share in this award with all of you. Indeed, the honor has been bestowed upon us as a direct result of your individual efforts and your dedication to our family atmosphere. This is an award that has been earned by every employee at Gold Star, and one that should make us all quite proud.

Over 130,000 Michigan employees were given anonymous surveys to complete on wide ranging topics related to their job. This marks the first year that the competition was open to the entire state, and I am proud of all of you for helping us retain our ranking as one of the best places to be in Michigan.

I continue to be moved on a daily basis by the individual efforts that I see from every one of you, and I often marvel at the great team that keeps us humming along. Our business volume has been high for the past several months and I realize that it can put a strain on a number of things, both professionally and personally. For these reasons I am all the more grateful to the family that we have built over the years -- a family that continues to grow. In this time of economic uncertainty it is critical that we maintain an upbeat atmosphere. While it is important to have systems, management, products, and business models to depend on, there is one thing that stands above the rest -- something that we all must rely on as we move into our bright future: each other.

Congratulations to all of you, and I look forward to growing and strengthening our family in the coming weeks, months, and years.

Dan Milstein

Here are just some of the employee comments from the Top Workplace survey.

Sample Survey Comments

"Several individuals here have many years worth of experience within the mortgage industry. As a result I have applied what I have learned from my colleagues to my interactions with my own clients..."

"I am able to wake up every single morning and be excited about going to work. The dynamic leadership is supportive and helps you expand your success."

"This company is run by people who are respected by their employees and they truly value their employees. This is an honest company that has done well because of the ethics and values it holds."

"Everyone here is held to a high standard. The support of the management allows us to keep a high level of performance. Also the company's culture calls for people to hold themselves to high standards."

Detroit Free Press

www.freep.com

615 W. Lafayette Bvd, Detroit, MI 48226 | Phone: 313-222-6606 | Fax: 313-222-8874 | panger@freepress.com

Paul Anger
Editor & Publisher

August 31, 2010

Gold Star Mortgage Financial Group
Dan Milstein
3879 Packard Road
Ann Arbor, MI 48108

**Detroit
Free
Press**

TOP
WORK
PLACES
2010

Dear Dan Milstein:

I'm very pleased to announce that Gold Star Mortgage Financial Group is a 2010 Detroit Free Press Top Workplace, based on a comprehensive analysis conducted by Workplace Dynamics. Please accept my congratulations for this outstanding accomplishment—it's well-deserved recognition as we all strive to move our region forward.

The companies included in the Detroit Free Press's Top Workplaces list were selected from a survey of employees measuring qualities such as company leadership, career opportunities, workplace flexibility, compensation and benefits. The rankings and overall results will be showcased in the Top Workplaces special section, to be published in the Free Press on Sunday, November 14.

In recognition of your accomplishments, we hope you and other representatives from your company can join us for a congratulatory breakfast on Thursday, November 11. You can celebrate the success you've had in creating a positive working environment and meet the other companies named as Top Workplaces. More details about this event will be sent to you in the coming weeks.

We will also send you a Top Workplace logo for your use in marketing communications.

Additionally, we invite you to promote your workplace in the Detroit Free Press Top Workplaces special section. For advertising opportunities please contact Scott Murray, Employment Sales Director, at 586-977-7577 or at shmurray@dnps.com by Friday, October 29.

We hope to see your company's representatives to be honored on November 11. Again,

Sincerely,

Paul Anger

Paul Anger

GANNETT

Letter announcing Gold Star Mortgage Financial Group's designation as a Detroit Free Press Top Workplace for 2010

Inc.5 0 5 0

Daniel Milstein   August 1, 2009
Gold Star Mortgage Financial Group
3879 Packard St
Ann Arbor, MI 48108-2011

Dear Daniel Milstein

On behalf of *Inc.* magazine, I am delighted to inform you that Gold Star Mortgage Financial Group has earned the position of 349 on the 2009 Inc. 500, Inc.'s annual ranking of the fastest-growing private companies in America.

Since debuting in 1991 with 100 of the fastest-growing private U.S. companies, then expanding the following year to the Inc. 500 and again in 2007 to the Inc. 5000, the list has served as evidence of the significant accomplishments of entrepreneurial companies. As an Inc. 500 honoree, Gold Star Mortgage Financial Group shares a prestigious pedigree with such notable alumni as Intuit, GoDaddy, Under Armour, Jamba Juice, Timberland, Clif Bar, Microsoft, Patagonia, American Apparel, Oracle and scores of other powerhouses.

Congratuations to you and your team. *Inc.* recognizes the creativity, dedication, and hard work that have gone into building Gold Star Mortgage Financial Group into what it is today and wishes you many more years of success.

Sincerely,

Jane Berenston

Jane Berenston
Editor
Inc. magazine

Letter of congratulations from *Inc.* Magazine, August 2009

Congratulations!

Daniel Milstein
Gold Star Mortgage Financial Group

Scotsman Guide is pleased to present Top Originators 2010, the industry's most comprehensive ranking of the mortgage industry's top producers. Roughly 700 entrants submitted their information for inclusion in the list, but only a select few made the cut in April 2011's residential edition of *Scotsman Guide*. These elite mortgage brokers, bankers, etc., are listed by loan volume, closed loans, Federal Housing Administration volume, purchase volume, refinance volume, and volume gain between 2009 and 2010.

Online rankings: scotsmanguide.com/Top2010

Reprinted with permission from Scotsman Guide Residential Edition and scotsmanguide.com, April 2011.

Top Dollar Volume

Online rankings: scotsmanguide.com/Top2010

#	Name	Company	State	Volume	Purchases Vs. Refis	Closed Loans
1	Daniel Milstein	Gold Star Mortgage Financial Group	MI	$385,491,680	36%/64%	1,209
2	Thomas Lavallee	Mortgage Bancorp Services	IL	$330,433,147	11%/89%	1,399
3	Suren Sampat	Advantage Mortgage Draper and Kramer Company	IL	$228,415,417	7%/93%	876
4	Shimmy Braun	Guaranteed Rate Inc.	IL	$225,769,806	25%/75%	722
5	Kevin Lyons	Anchor Funding Inc.	CA	$220,911,573	20%/80%	677
6	Christopher Vincent Hussain	WeFit2U Inc.	CA	$195,132,018	70%/30%	590
7	Harinder Johar	Guaranteed Rate Inc.	IL	$194,025,187	14%/86%	592
8	Brad Cohen	EagleBank	MD	$190,529,089	14%/86%	513
9	David Jaffe	On Q Financial Inc.	CA	$189,106,724	21%/79%	493
10	John Vlogianitis	Wells Fargo Home Mortgage	NY	$185,815,430	47%/53%	463
11	Tom Digan	Mortgage Master Inc.	MA	$183,246,763	17%/83%	500
12	Yinan Nancy Sun	Austin First Mortgage	TX	$178,931,636	14%/86%	896
13	Norman Calvo	Universal Mortgage Inc.	NY	$178,222,556	49%/51%	382
14	Paul Volpe	NOVA Home Loans	AZ	$172,151,323	46%/54%	827
15	Al Hensling	United American Mortgage	CA	$170,176,169	31%/69%	365
16	Brian Scott Cohen	Wells Fargo Home Mortgage	NY	$170,067,792	53%/47%	409
17	Joe Caltabiano	Guaranteed Rate Inc.	IL	$168,231,056	32%/68%	447
18	Tim Roach	Trident Mortgage Co.	PA	$165,536,494	50%/50%	485
19	Richard Faust	Bank of America Home Loans	CA	$164,440,436	27%/73%	280
20	Anthony Musante	Bank of America Home Loans	CA	$162,060,047	25%/75%	315
21	Gerry McCarthy	Mortgage Master Inc.	MA	$148,166,786	12%/88%	413
22	Brian Minkow	Prospect Mortgage	CA	$144,905,746	39%/61%	403
23	Dave Gibbs	Mortgage Master Inc.	MA	$142,796,271	12%/88%	477
24	Michael Meena	Augusta Financial Inc.	CA	$141,492,028	54%/46%	423
25	Michael Shane	Sammamish Mortgage	WA	$140,859,386	12%/88%	480
26	Deborah O'Rourke	Mortgage Master Inc.	MA	$137,111,518	16%/84%	419
27	Kevin Budde	Bank of America Home Loans	CA	$136,816,835	66%/34%	353
28	Michael Bischof	Biltmore Financial Bancorp Inc.	IL	$134,351,202	20%/80%	408
29	Carl Nielsen	Mortgage Master Inc.	MA	$129,869,536	41%/59%	351
30	John Willis	Mortgage Master Inc.	MA	$128,231,670	14%/86%	435
31	Alison Freed	Mortgage Master Inc.	MA	$127,733,798	11%/89%	350

Top Dollar Volume

#	Name	Company	State	Volume	Purchases Vs. Refis	Closed Loans
1	Daniel Milstein	Gold Star Mortgage Financial Group	MI	$374,150,340	64% / 36%	1,049
2	Thomas Lavallee	Mortgage Bancorp Services	IL	$287,270,050	30% / 70%	1,162
3	John Vlogianitis	Wells Fargo Home Mortgage				
4	Shimmy Braun	Guaranteed Rate Inc.				
5	Paul Volpe	NOVA Home Loans				
6	Joseph Smith	Bank of America Home Loans				
7	Kevin Lyons	Anchor Funding Inc.				
8	Michael Daversa	Atlantic Residential Mortgage				
9	Thomas Digan	Mortgage Master Inc.				
10	Gerald McCarthy	Mortgage Master Inc.				
11	Al Hensling	United American Mortgage Co				
12	Brad Cohen	Embrace Home Loans Inc.				
13	Alison Freed	Mortgage Master Inc.				
14	Tim Roach	Trident Mortgage Co.				
15	Yinan Nancy Sun	Austin First Mortgage				
16	Deborah O'Rourke	Mortgage Master Inc.				
17	David Jaffe	On Q Financial Inc.				
18	David Gibbs	Mortgage Master Inc.				
19	Joe Caltabiano	Guaranteed Rate Inc.				
20	Michael Bischof	Biltmore Financial Bancorp Inc				
21	Mehdi Pirzadeh	Embrace Home Loans Inc.				
22	Amanda Sessa	WR Starkey Mortgage				
23	Mark Klein	Pacific Coast Lending				
24	John Farrell	Bank of America Home Loans				
25	Joe Phalen	Wintrust Mortgage Corp.				
26	Jon Levin	Wells Fargo Home Mortgage				
27	Mike Meena	Augusta Financial Inc.				
28	Jim Bane	WR Starkey Mortgage				
29	John Willis	Mortgage Master Inc.				
30	Rod Flowers	SunTrust Mortgage Inc.				
31	Sherry Zickert	U.S. Bank Home Mortgage				
32	Norman Calvo	Universal Mortgage Inc.				
33	Kathy Shaw	First Place Bank				
34	Brian Blonder	JBL Mortgage Network	MD	$105,075,251	10% / 90%	333

2009 Top Overall Volume

Closed-Loans Rank: #2 | Purchase-Volume Rank: #1

Daniel Milstein
Gold Star Mortgage Financial Group

Daniel Milstein ranks No. 1 on *Scotsman Guide*'s Top Originators 2009 list by volume with $374 million. He also closed 1,049 loans, averaging more than $350,000 for each. To achieve the top spot, Milstein maintained a frenetic pace — but he didn't get there overnight.

As president and CEO of Gold Star Mortgage in Ann Arbor, Mich., Milstein has evolved his base from that of a predominantly Michigan market — including Big Three auto workers, foreign buyers and professional hockey players — to a multistate network of customers in his home state, Arizona, Connecticut, Florida and Texas.

Milstein can handle a $2.5 million mortgage, he says. But he noted his typical loan is much smaller. In fact, after subtracting "celebrity customers" — such as professional athletes, team owners and company CEOs — his average loan is $212,000, he says.

Although he has one full-time assistant and one part-timer — plus a marketing and public-relations coordinator — Milstein takes all of the initial applications.

"I discuss the rate and loan, get approval and submit it to the lender and then hand the file to an assistant," he says.

All that translates into what Milstein estimates as an 80-hour work week.

"I'm usually the first one here and last to leave," he says. "I've always got two phones and a Blackberry with me." (DR)

2009 M.O.M. TOP 200 ORIGINATORS
Number of Loans (2008)

	Name	Company	State	Loans	$ Volume	Broker/ Banker	% Purchase	% Refi	No. Ass
1	Melissa Cohn	The Manhattan Mortgage Company	NY	1016	$885,328,687	Broker	60	40	
2	Rodney Anderson	Rodney Anderson Lending Services	TX	897	$143,912,871	Banker	80	20	
3	Daniel Milstein	Gold Star Mortgage Financial Group	MI	803	$278,620,645	Both	68	32	
4	Shawn Portmann	Benchmark Mortgage	WA	754	$202,585,067	Banker	90	10	
5	Mark Cohen	Cohen Financial Group	CA	709	$751,656,166	Banker	47	53	
6	Thomas Lavallee	Mortgage Bancorp Services	IL	668	$171,630,242	Broker	25	75	
7	James Pope	M&I Bank	WI	591	$140,725,391	Banker	54	46	
8	Jon Volpe	NOVA Home Loans	AZ	508	$134,182,376	Both	55	45	
9	Jody Cooper	Wells Fargo Home Mortgage	CO	501	$217,076,460	Banker	48	52	
10	Dennis Duncan	SunTrust Mortgage, Inc.	VA	443	$69,808,113	Banker	75	25	
11	John Rodgers	Prime Mortgage Lending	NC	438	$82,993,521	Broker	64	36	
12	Linda Mister	WR Starkey Mortgage	TX	424	$63,139,880	Banker	89	11	
13	Shawn Huss	National City Mortgage	OH	421	$64,210,048	Banker	52	48	
14	James Nesbit	National City Mortgage	WA	418	$89,152,229	Banker	30	70	
15	Paul Volpe	NOVA Home Loans	AZ	415	$89,376,892	Both	60	40	
16	Shimmy Braun	Guaranteed Rate	IL	413	$124,339,154	Both	43	57	
17	Joe Phalen	Wintrust Mortgage	IL	410	$102,620,279	Both	49	51	
18	Jerry Sundt	Sundt Mortgage Group	AZ	400	$86,222,600	Broker	70	30	
19	Rod Flowers	SunTrust Mortgage, Inc.	MD	395	$79,080,990	Banker	50	50	
20	Jeff Crothers	National City Mortgage	CA	392	$90,571,527	Banker	67	33	
21	Jim Bane	WR Starkey Mortgage	TX	390	$67,514,301	Banker	79	21	
22	Rick Richter	Gold Star Financial	MI	386	$89,091,845	Broker	41	59	
23	Keith Thompson	National City Mortgage	IL	384	$46,162,601	Banker	64	36	
24	John Abraham	National City Mortgage	IL	376	$63,256,973	Banker	70	30	
25	Matt Elerding	Chase Home Mortgage	WA	367	$59,146,000	Banker	47	53	
26	Kevin Lyons	Anchor Funding Inc	CA	366	$119,636,051	Both	15	85	
27	Mark Lewin	MetLife Home Loans	IN	366	$55,157,502	Banker	80	20	
28	Larry Cohen	Trident Mortgage Company	PA	363	$117,427,681	Banker	82	18	
29	Steven Siwinski	BancGROUP Mortgage Coproration	IL	360	$83,282,305	Both	50	50	
30	Joseph Meehan	Guaranteed Rate	IL	359	$112,783,853	Both	50	50	
31	Michael Berrodin	PHH Mortgage	NJ	351	$79,512,962	Banker	75	25	
32	Michael Daversa	Atlantic Residential Mortgage	CT	348	$184,715,340	Broker	67	33	
33	Jeffrey Slater	BancGROUP Mortgage Coproration	IL	348	$78,761,225	Both	62	38	
34	Mike Meena	Augusta Financial	CA	345	$103,874,194	Broker	76	24	
35	Tom Roth	National City Mortgage	IL	344	$51,578,970	Banker	56	44	
36	Tim Roach	Trident Mortgage Company	PA	335	$115,171,708	Banker	74	26	
37	Thomas Digan	Mortgage Master, Inc.	MA	312	$127,451,644	Both	27	73	
38	Jim Rademann	R and R Mortgage	CA	306	$104,567,000	Broker	75	45	
39	Scott Dillon	National City Mortgage	IL	303	$39,540,559	Banker	58	42	
40	Susan Moore	WR Starkey Mortgage	TX	301	$42,180,975	Banker	99	1	
41	Kelly Novotny	Union Bank & Trust Company	NE	299	$57,124,481	Banker	42	58	
42	Jack Overy	MetLife Home Loans	IN	296	$40,328,127	Banker	90	10	

Reprinted from April 2009 issue of Mortgage Originator Magazine, with Permission from Summit Business Media/ Source Media.

About the Author
Daniel Milstein

K NOWN AS A FINANCIAL wizard with solid experience planning and managing diversified real estate loan portfolios for companies and individuals, Dan Milstein has an uncanny ability to sense shifting market conditions and respond quickly and efficiently for his clients. With a strong foundation in all phases of loan origination, there isn't a problem or loan scenario that Dan hasn't come across. He is well versed in all areas of consumer lending including fraud prevention, quality control, state and federal regulations, credit-risk policies, accounting, finance and marketing.

Dan is currently the #1 ranked loan officer in the United States out of 550,000 originators in the industry, a title he has held for two consecutive years and counting. He has been ranked in the top 10 nationally and worldwide every year for the last decade.

His extensive research of both domestic and foreign financial markets, as well as a thorough understanding of the fluctuations of business has helped him shepherd his company and clients through the financial crisis.

But what truly motivates him to continue pursuing business success is his sense of loyalty to his more than 400 employees and more than 1,500 family members who depend on Gold Star's stability. Daniel has always expressed a deep desire to stay true to his staff and their families, business partners, and colleagues.

Dan's leadership is the main reason Gold Star Mortgage is:

- One of *Inc. Magazine*'s 500 fastest growing companies in America for two consecutive years (2009-2010), as well as the 14th fastest growing company in the financial services sector.

- The third Largest Residential Lender in Michigan and 53rd largest in the United States.

- A Detroit Free Press Top Work Place in Michigan for employees in 2009 and again 2010.

- A quickly growing company currently employing over 400 people in 25 offices.

- Slated to open several new offices in 2011 and beyond.

- A successful company, with a 730% growth volume between 2005 and 2009.

Born in Kiev, Ukraine, Dan and his family relocated to the United States in 1991. He received his bachelor's degree with honors in business management and finance. With his knowledge of the industry firmly in place, he found himself quickly moving up the ranks of the banking industry. He worked his way up from assistant consumer lending manager, to general manager, to underwriter, to Chief Operating Officer and finally Chief Executive Officer within various financial institutions.

Dan also gives back to his community, serving on the Cleary University Board of Trustees, as well as a board member of several corporations. He is widely viewed as an expert in the industry and has published numerous articles and essays on banking and finance in several publications.

Index

www.abcofsales.com